# CONTINENTS IN CLOSE-UP

# NORTH AMERICA

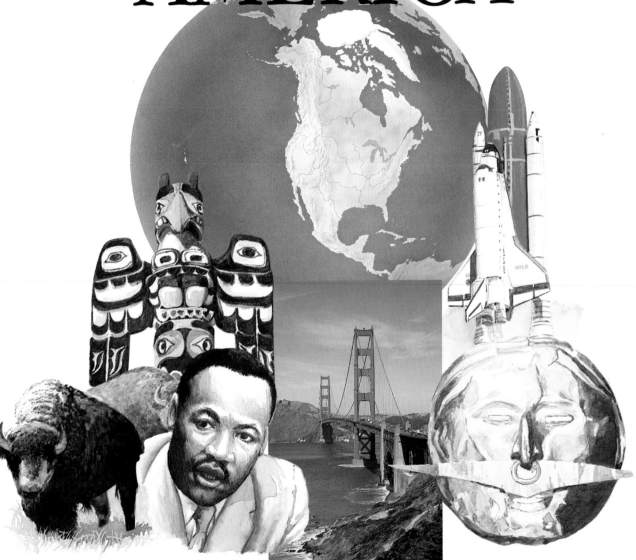

## MALCOLM PORTER and KEITH LYE

### CHERRYTREE BOOKS

A Cherrytree Book

Designed and produced by
AS Publishing
Text by Keith Lye

First published 1999
by Cherrytree Press Limited
a subsidiary of
The Chivers Company Limited
Windsor Bridge Road
Bath BA2 3AX

Copyright © Malcolm Porter and AS Publishing

British Library Cataloguing in Publication data

Porter, Malcolm
    North America. - (continents in close-up)
    1.Children's atlases
    2.North America - Maps for children
    I.Title II.Lye, Keith
    912.7

ISBN 0 7540 9035 3

Printed in Italy by L. E. G. O.

# CONTINENTS IN CLOSE-UP

# NORTH AMERICA

This illustrated atlas combines maps, pictures, flags, globes,
information panels, diagrams and charts to give an overview
of the whole continent and a closer look at each of its countries.

## COUNTRY CLOSE-UPS

Each double-page spread has these
features:

**Introduction** The author introduces the
most important facts about the country
or region.

**Globes** A globe on which you can see the
country's position in the continent and the
world.

**Flags** Every country's flag is shown.

**Information panels** Every country has an
information panel which gives its area,
population and capital, and where
possible its currency, religions, languages,
main towns and government.

**Pictures** Important features of each
country are illustrated and captioned to
give a flavour of the country. You can
find out about physical features, famous
people, ordinary people, animals, plants,
places, products and much more.

**Maps** Every country is shown on a
clear, accurate map. To get the most out
of the maps it helps to know the symbols
which are shown in the key on the
opposite page.

**Land** You can see by the colouring on
the map where the land is forested,
frozen or desert.

**Height** Relief hill shading shows where
the mountain ranges are. Individual
mountains are marked by a triangle.

**Direction** All of the maps are drawn
with north at the top of the page.

**Scale** All of the maps are drawn to scale
so that you can find the distance
between places in miles or kilometres.

```
0                           200 miles
├──────────┼──────────┤
0              200 kilometres
```

# KEY TO MAPS

| | |
|---|---|
| **CANADA** | Country name |
| TEXAS | Province or state name |
| ⌒ | Country border |
| ■ | More than 1 million people* |
| ● | More than 500,000 people |
| • | Less than 500,000 people |
| □ | Country capital |
| ★ | State or province capital |
| ROCKY MTS | Mountain range |
| ▲ Mt McKinley 6194m | Mountain with its height |
| ∴ Tikal | Archaeological site |

| | |
|---|---|
| *Ohio* | River |
| | Canal |
| | Lake |
| | Dam |
| | Island |

| | |
|---|---|
| | Forest |
| | Crops |
| | Dry grassland |
| | Desert |
| | Tundra |
| | Polar |

*Many large cities, such as Boston, have metropolitan populations that are greater than the city figures. Such cities have larger dot sizes to emphasize their importance.*

## CONTINENT CLOSE-UPS

**People and Beliefs** Map of population densities; chart of percentage of population per country; chart of areas of countries; map of religions; chart of main religious groups.

**Climate and Vegetation** Map of vegetation from polar to desert; map of winter and summer temperatures; map of annual rainfall; diagram of mountain climates.

**Ecology and Environment** Map of environmental problems and disasters; map of earthquake zones, volcanoes, hurricanes and tornadoes; diagram of greenhouse effect; panel of endangered animals and plants.

**Economy** Map of agricultural and industrial products; chart of gross national products for individual countries; panel on per capita gross national products; map of sources of energy.

**Politics and History** Map of political systems; panel of great events; timeline of important dates; panel showing Viking longship and Voyager space probe; map of location of major events in North American history.

---

**Index** All the names on the maps and in the picture captions can be found in the index at the end of the book.

# CONTENTS

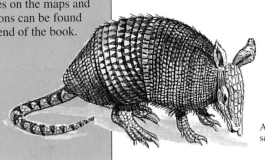

Armadillo
see page 18

# NORTH AMERICA

North America is the third largest continent after Asia and Africa. The two biggest countries, Canada and the United States, are among the world's richest. These two high-income countries have many high-tech industries and most people enjoy comfortable lives. Mexico and the countries of Central America and the Caribbean are low- or middle-income countries. Many of their people are poor.

The climate of North America varies greatly from north to south. A huge ice sheet covers most of Greenland in the northeast, with smaller ice caps in northern Canada. The southern parts of North America lie in the hot and humid tropics.

ALASKA (US)

PACIFIC OCEAN

**Whales** swim off the west coast of North America and people enjoy watching them. Many North Americans believe that the development of the land and sea should be controlled so that wildlife and natural wonders can be conserved.

**Golden Gate Bridge** in San Francisco, California, is one of North America's most famous landmarks. San Francisco was rebuilt after a great earthquake in 1906. Earthquakes and volcanic eruptions occur in western North America and in the Caribbean.

**Market days**, where farmers sell their produce and buy goods for their families, are important events in Central America. Farming employs more than 30 per cent of the people of tropical North America. Many farmers are poor and struggle to survive.

**Combine harvesters** are used on the huge cereal farms of Canada and the United States. Farming is highly mechanized here and employs only three per cent of the people. The farms are, however, much more productive than those in the countries to the south.

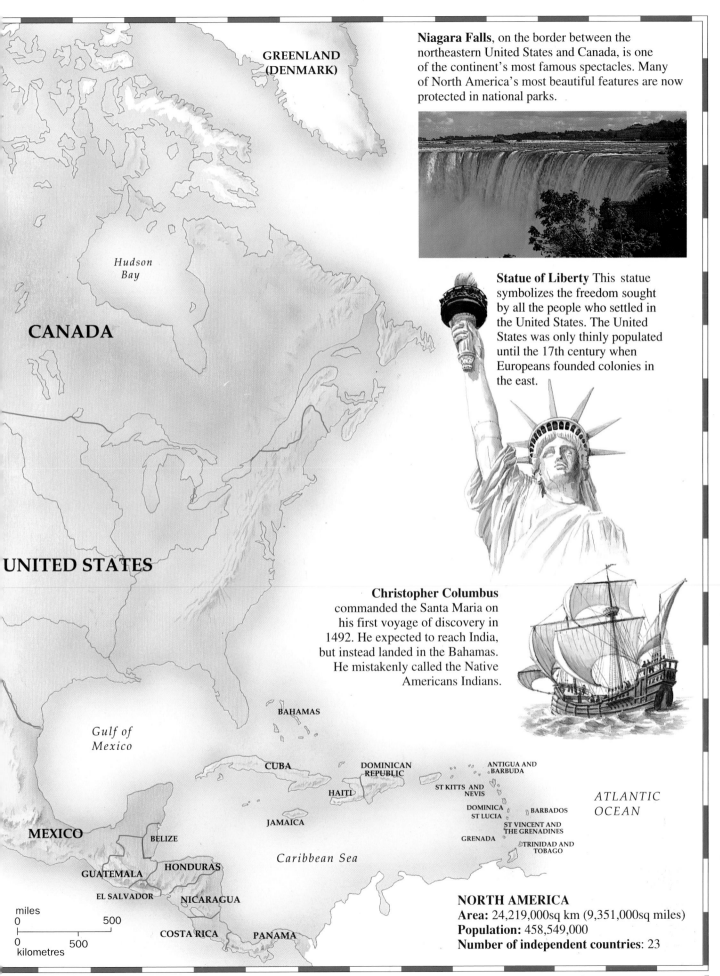

**GREENLAND (DENMARK)**

**Niagara Falls**, on the border between the northeastern United States and Canada, is one of the continent's most famous spectacles. Many of North America's most beautiful features are now protected in national parks.

**Statue of Liberty** This statue symbolizes the freedom sought by all the people who settled in the United States. The United States was only thinly populated until the 17th century when Europeans founded colonies in the east.

*Hudson Bay*

**CANADA**

**UNITED STATES**

**Christopher Columbus** commanded the Santa Maria on his first voyage of discovery in 1492. He expected to reach India, but instead landed in the Bahamas. He mistakenly called the Native Americans Indians.

BAHAMAS

*Gulf of Mexico*

CUBA

DOMINICAN REPUBLIC

ANTIGUA AND BARBUDA

ST KITTS AND NEVIS

HAITI

DOMINICA

ST LUCIA

BARBADOS

*ATLANTIC OCEAN*

JAMAICA

ST VINCENT AND THE GRENADINES

GRENADA

TRINIDAD AND TOBAGO

**MEXICO**

BELIZE

*Caribbean Sea*

GUATEMALA

HONDURAS

EL SALVADOR

NICARAGUA

miles
0          500

0          500
kilometres

COSTA RICA

PANAMA

**NORTH AMERICA**
**Area:** 24,219,000sq km (9,351,000sq miles)
**Population:** 458,549,000
**Number of independent countries:** 23

# CANADA AND GREENLAND

Canada is the world's second largest country. Only Russia is bigger. Much of Canada has long, bitterly cold winters and most Canadians live within 320 km (200 miles) of the southern border with the United States. The first people to live in Canada were Native Americans. But most Canadians today are descendants of French and British settlers.

Greenland is the world's largest island. It is a self-governing part of Denmark.

## CANADA

**Area:** 9,976,139sq km (3,851,809sq miles)
**Highest point:** Mount Logan, 6,050m (19,849ft)
**Population:** 29,964,000
**Capital:** Ottawa (pop 312,000)
**Largest cities:** Toronto (4,264,000)
Montreal (3,327,000)
Vancouver (1,832,000)
**Official languages:** English, French
**Religions:** Roman Catholic 45%, Protestant 36%, Eastern Orthodox 2%, other 17%
**Government:** Federal constitutional monarchy
**Currency:** Canadian dollar

## GREENLAND
**Area:** 2,175,600sq km (840,000 sq miles)
**Population:** 58,000
**Capital:** Godthaab
**Government:** Self-governing part of Denmark

## ST PIERRE & MIQUELON
**Area:** 242sq km (93sq miles)
**Population:** 6,000
**Capital:** St Pierre
**Government:** French territory

Beaufort Sea

Melville Island
Banks Island
Bathurst Island
Some Isla
Prince of Wales Island
Victoria Island
King Willia Islan

Dawson

Mackenzie

Coppermine

Great Bear Lake

YUKON TERRITORY
▲ Mount Logan 6050m
★ Whitehorse

NORTHWEST TERRITORIES

Yellowknife ★

Great Slave Lake

C A N

BRITISH COLUMBIA

Peace

Lake Athabasca

Fort St John

R O C K Y

Queen Charlotte Islands

Prince Rupert

M O U N T A I N S

PACIFIC OCEAN

Prince George

ALBERTA

Athabasca

Churchill

MANITO

Edmonton ★

SASKATCHEWAN

Prince Albert ★

Lak Winnip

Vancouver Island

Fraser

Calgary

Saskatchewan

Saskatoon

**Vancouver**

Victoria

Medicine Hat

Regina ★

Winnip

Brandon

**Rail transport** was important in opening up the vast country of Canada. The two major companies are the government-owned Canadian National Railways (CN) and the privately owned Canadian Pacific (CP) Rail System.

**Rocky Mountains** This vast range in western Canada has much magnificent scenery. The Pacific Ranges rise to the west of the Rockies. Canada's highest peak, Mount Logan, is in the northwest.

**GREENLAND (DENMARK)**

*llesmere Island*

*Baffin Bay*

Disko Island

*on Island*

*Baffin Island*

Godthaab

A V U T

Iqaluit

*Southampton Island*

0    250 miles

0    250 kilometres

D A

*Hudson Bay*

*Ungava Peninsula*

Nain

*ATLANTIC OCEAN*

*NEWFOUNDLAND*

*Labrador*

hurchill

St John's

*Newfoundland*

**St Pierre & Miquelon (FRANCE)**

QUEBEC

*Anticosti Island*

Glace Bay

Fort Albany

Chicoutimi

PRINCE EDWARD ISLAND

NEW BRUNSWICK

★ Charlottetown

NOVA SCOTIA

ONTARIO

Fredericton

*St Lawrence*

Quebec

Saint John

Halifax

Trois Rivières

Thunder Bay

**Montreal**

*Lake Superior*

Sault Ste Marie

**Ottawa**

Oshawa

*Lake Huron*

**Toronto** ★

*Lake Ontario*

*Lake Michigan*

Kitchener

London

*Lake Erie*

Windsor

**Inuit** These people live in northern Canada, especially in the new territory of Nunavut. Traditionally the Inuit lived by fishing and hunting whales and seals, but of the 36,000 that survive, most have given up their old way of life.

**CN Tower** This communications and observation tower in Toronto is the world's tallest free-standing structure at 553 m (1,815 ft) high. Toronto, which stands on Lake Ontario, has Canada's largest metropolitan area population.

**Maple leaf** This is Canada's national symbol. Golden-brown maple syrup and sugar are made from the sap of the sugar maple tree. Maple syrup is an important product in Ontario and Quebec. People spread it on waffles for their breakfast.

# EASTERN CANADA

The four Atlantic provinces, together with Ontario and Quebec, make up eastern Canada. This region covers less than a third of Canada, but it contains about 70 per cent of the country's population. The most densely populated area extends along the shores of lakes Erie and Ontario and through the St Lawrence River valley. The river itself, together with several lakes, canals and locks, form a major waterway called the St Lawrence Seaway. This waterway is the outlet for the entire Great Lakes region.

**Seals** are found around the coasts of eastern Canada. Hunting of newborn harp seals for their fur has now been stopped.

**Samuel de Champlain,** a French explorer, helped to colonize French Canada in the early 17th century. Many Canadians still speak French, especially in the province of Quebec.

**Beavers** live in rivers and lakes in forested regions throughout eastern Canada. They gnaw down trees and use branches to build dams and lodges (homes) for their young in the water.

**Hockey,** also called ice hockey, is Canada's national sport. This fast and exciting game played on an ice rink began in Canada in the mid-19th century and it is now played by many countries.

*Ungava Peninsula*

*Hudson Bay*

*James Bay*

Fort Albany

ONTARIO

Kenora

Timmins

Thunder Bay

*Lake Superior*

Sault Ste Marie

*Lake Huron*

*Lake Michigan*

**Toronto** ★  *Lake Ontario*

Kitchener

Hamilton

*Niagara Falls*

London

*Lake Erie*

Windsor

0           200 miles

0           200 kilometres

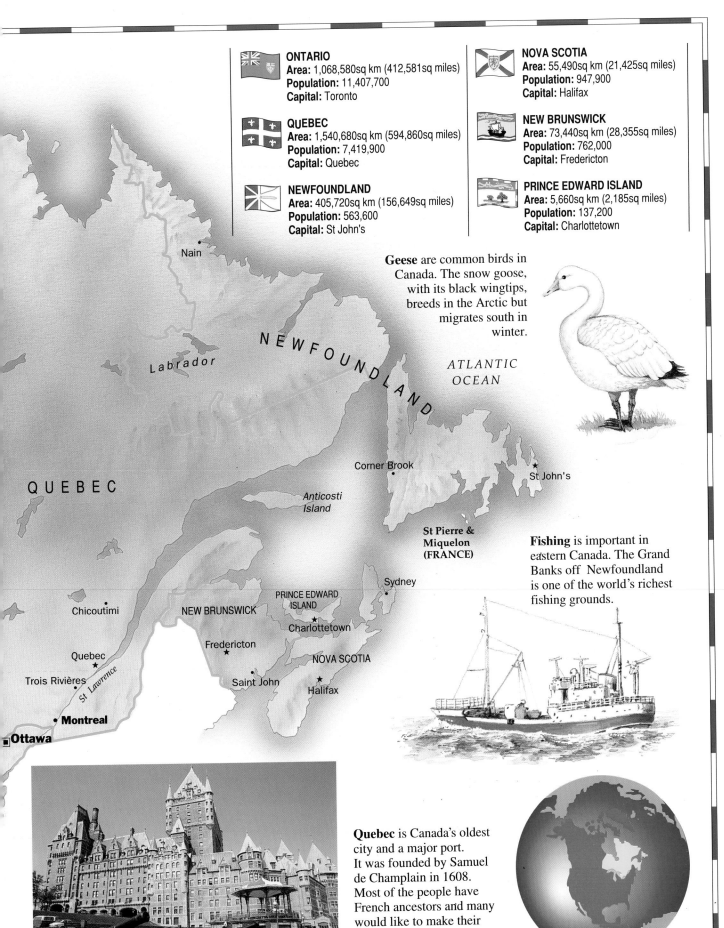

**ONTARIO**
**Area:** 1,068,580sq km (412,581sq miles)
**Population:** 11,407,700
**Capital:** Toronto

**QUEBEC**
**Area:** 1,540,680sq km (594,860sq miles)
**Population:** 7,419,900
**Capital:** Quebec

**NEWFOUNDLAND**
**Area:** 405,720sq km (156,649sq miles)
**Population:** 563,600
**Capital:** St John's

**NOVA SCOTIA**
**Area:** 55,490sq km (21,425sq miles)
**Population:** 947,900
**Capital:** Halifax

**NEW BRUNSWICK**
**Area:** 73,440sq km (28,355sq miles)
**Population:** 762,000
**Capital:** Fredericton

**PRINCE EDWARD ISLAND**
**Area:** 5,660sq km (2,185sq miles)
**Population:** 137,200
**Capital:** Charlottetown

Nain

NEWFOUNDLAND

Labrador

ATLANTIC OCEAN

**Geese** are common birds in Canada. The snow goose, with its black wingtips, breeds in the Arctic but migrates south in winter.

QUEBEC

Corner Brook

St John's

Anticosti Island

**St Pierre & Miquelon (FRANCE)**

Sydney

Chicoutimi

PRINCE EDWARD ISLAND

NEW BRUNSWICK

Charlottetown

Fredericton

NOVA SCOTIA

Quebec

Trois Rivières

St Lawrence

Saint John

Halifax

• Montreal

Ottawa

**Fishing** is important in eastern Canada. The Grand Banks off Newfoundland is one of the world's richest fishing grounds.

**Quebec** is Canada's oldest city and a major port. It was founded by Samuel de Champlain in 1608. Most of the people have French ancestors and many would like to make their province a separate French-speaking country.

# WESTERN CANADA

Western Canada consists of four provinces – Alberta, British Columbia, Manitoba and Saskatchewan – and three territories – Northwest Territories, Nunavut, which was created in 1999, and Yukon Territory. The provinces contain vast plains called prairies, towering mountains in the west, and the Pacific coast. The three territories in the north are thinly populated. Less than one in a hundred Canadians lives there.

**Mounties** Officially called the Royal Canadian Mounted Police, the Mounties once rode on horseback across vast, thinly populated areas in pursuit of criminals. Today, they usually use motor vehicles but still 'get their man'.

**Vancouver** is western Canada's largest city. It is also Canada's leading port and the western terminal of the Canadian Pacific Rail System and Canadian National Railways. Food processing and the manufacture of wood products are its leading industries.

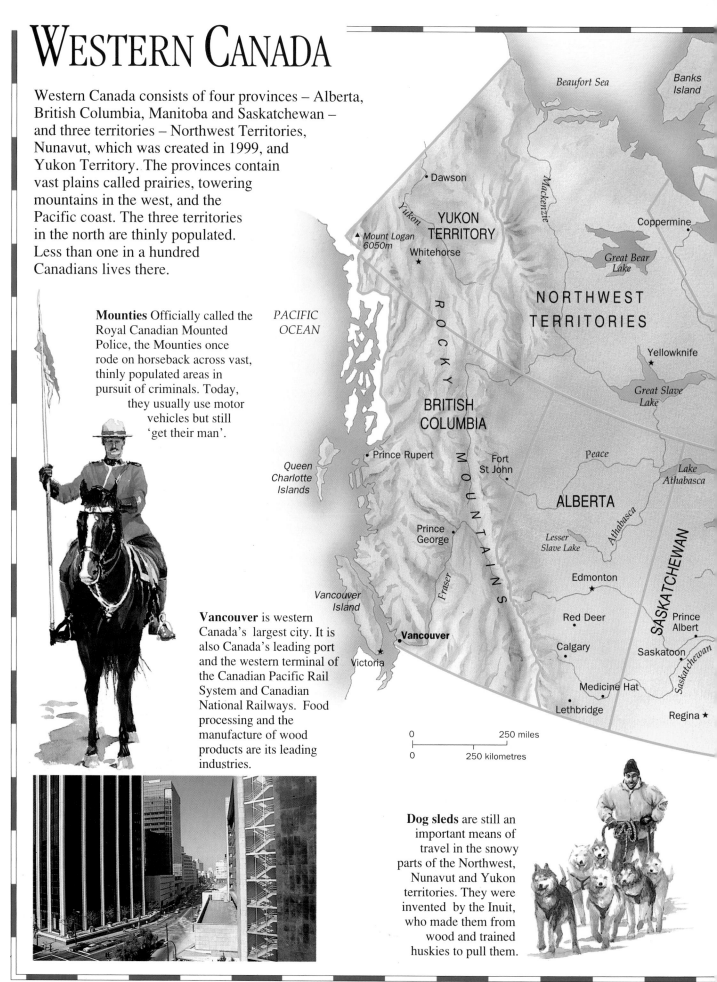

Beaufort Sea

Banks Island

Dawson

Mackenzie

YUKON TERRITORY

Coppermine

▲ Mount Logan 6050m

Whitehorse ★

Great Bear Lake

NORTHWEST TERRITORIES

PACIFIC OCEAN

Yellowknife ★

R O C K Y

Great Slave Lake

BRITISH COLUMBIA

Prince Rupert

Fort St John

Peace

Lake Athabasca

Queen Charlotte Islands

M O U N T A I N S

ALBERTA

Athabasca

SASKATCHEWAN

Prince George

Lesser Slave Lake

Edmonton ★

Fraser

Red Deer

Prince Albert

Vancouver Island

Calgary

Saskatoon

Saskatchewan

Vancouver ★

Victoria ★

Medicine Hat

Lethbridge

Regina ★

| 0 | 250 miles |
| 0 | 250 kilometres |

**Dog sleds** are still an important means of travel in the snowy parts of the Northwest, Nunavut and Yukon territories. They were invented by the Inuit, who made them from wood and trained huskies to pull them.

10

**ALBERTA**
**Area:** 661,190sq km (255,287sq miles)
**Population:** 2,847,000
**Capital:** Edmonton

**BRITISH COLUMBIA**
**Area:** 947,800sq km (365,948sq miles)
**Population:** 3,933,000
**Capital:** Victoria

**MANITOBA**
**Area:** 649,950sq km (250,947sq miles)
**Population:** 1,145,200
**Capital:** Winnipeg

**SASKATCHEWAN**
**Area:** 652,330sq km (251,866sq miles)
**Population:** 1,023,500
**Capital:** Regina

**NORTHWEST TERRITORIES**
**Area:** 1,224,920sq km (472,945sq miles)
**Population:** 45,500
**Capital:** Yellowknife

**NUNAVUT**
**Area:** 2,201,400sq km (849,965sq miles)
**Population:** 22,000
**Capital:** Iqaluit

**YUKON**
**Area:** 483,450sq km (186,661sq miles)
**Population:** 31,600
**Capital:** Whitehorse

**Polar bears** live on the northern coasts of Canada and in Greenland. Their numbers have declined because they have been hunted for their valuable pelts. Canada and other countries are now trying to protect them.

**Totem poles** These large wood carvings of animals or other natural objects are symbols of families or groups of Native Americans. The most spectacular are found along the Pacific coast of Canada.

**Forests**, mostly coniferous, are one of Canada's many natural resources. Canada is a leading producer of timber and it also exports many minerals. It produces oil and natural gas, together with copper, gold, iron ore, nickel, uranium and zinc.

11

# UNITED STATES OF AMERICA

The United States is the world's fourth largest country but, in population, ranks third. The country consists of 50 states, 48 of which form a large block between Canada and Mexico. The 49th state, Alaska, lies in the far northwest of North America, while the 50th, Hawaii, is a chain of volcanic islands in the North Pacific Ocean. The United States also includes the District of Columbia, where the capital Washington DC is located.

**George Washington,** the first president of the United States (1789-97), led the Continental Army against the British in the American War of Independence, or RevolutionaryWar, (1775-83). Its victory led to the birth of the United States.

**Native Americans** were the first people to live in what is now the United States. They crossed from Asia into North America at least 10,000 years ago.

**Landscapes** The United States has large forests, grasslands, snow-capped mountains and deserts. Much of the scenery is spectacular. Monument Valley on the Utah-Arizona border contains these remarkable rock formations.

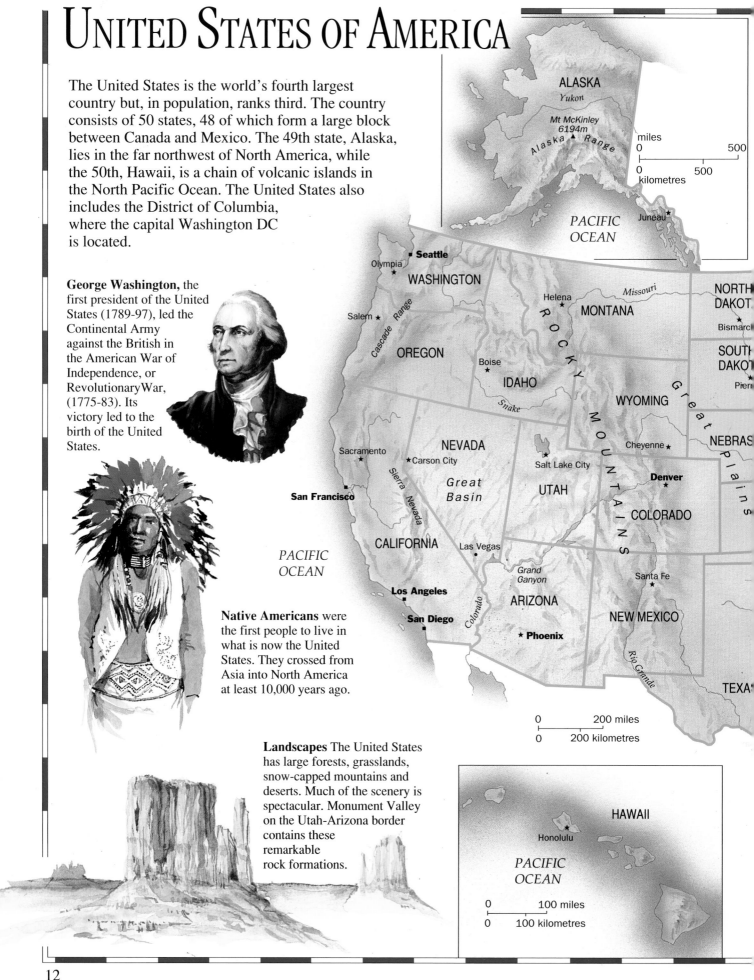

ALASKA
Yukon
Mt McKinley 6194m
Alaska Range
miles 0   500
0   500 kilometres
PACIFIC OCEAN
Juneau

Seattle
Olympia
WASHINGTON
Helena
MONTANA
Missouri
NORTH DAKOT
Bismarc
Salem
Cascade Range
OREGON
Boise
IDAHO
Snake
SOUTH DAKOT
Pier
ROCKY
WYOMING
Great Plains
Sacramento
NEVADA
Carson City
Salt Lake City
Cheyenne
NEBRAS
San Francisco
Sierra Nevada
Great Basin
UTAH
Denver
COLORADO
MOUNTAINS
CALIFORNIA
Las Vegas
Grand Ganyon
Santa Fe
PACIFIC OCEAN
Los Angeles
San Diego
Colorado
ARIZONA
Phoenix
NEW MEXICO
Rio Grande
TEXA

0   200 miles
0   200 kilometres

HAWAII
Honolulu
PACIFIC OCEAN
0   100 miles
0   100 kilometres

# UNITED STATES

**Capital:** Washington DC (pop 543,000 )
**Largest cities:** New York City (7,381,000)
Los Angeles (3,554,000)
Chicago (2,722,000)
**Official language:** None (English is the chief
language spoken in the United States,
followed by Spanish)
**Religions:** Protestant 58%, Roman Catholic 21%,
other Christians 6.4%, Jews 2.1%, Muslims 1.9%
**Government:** Federal republic
**Currency:** United States dollar

**Area:** 9,529,063sq km
(3,679,192sq miles)
**Highest point:** Mount McKinley,
6,194m (20,320ft)
**Population:** 265,284,000

**Bald eagle** This
majestic bird of
prey was adopted as
the national bird in 1782.
Overhunting, pollution and
the destruction of wilderness
areas threatened its survival,
but it is now protected.

MAINE
Augusta ★

Montpelier ★
NEW
HAMPSHIRE
VERMONT ★ Concord
★ **Boston**
MASS.
Albany ★ Hartford ★ Providence
★ CONN. R.I.

Lake Superior

MINNESOTA

St Paul ★

MICHIGAN

Lake
Huron

Lake Ontario

NEW YORK

WISCONSIN

Lake
Michigan

Madison ★ **Milwaukee**

**Detroit** ★
Lansing ★ Lake
Erie

PENNSYLVANIA

■ **New York City**
★ Trenton
Harrisburg ★ **Philadelphia**
NEW JERSEY
Dover ■
DELAWARE

IOWA

**Chicago** ■

OHIO

**Washington DC** ■
★ Annapolis
MARYLAND

Des Moines ★

ILLINOIS
Springfield ★

INDIANA
**Columbus** ★
**Cincinnati** ■
**Indianapolis** ★

WEST
VIRGINIA

VIRGINIA
★
Charleston ★ Richmond

ite
ncoln ★

Mississippi

**Kansas City**
**St Louis** ■

Ohio

★ Frankfort

opeka ★
Jefferson City ★

MISSOURI

KENTUCKY

Nashville ★

Tennessee

Appalachian Mts

★ Raleigh
NORTH CAROLINA

*ATLANTIC
OCEAN*

ANSAS

OKLAHOMA

ARKANSAS

TENNESSEE

Columbia ★
SOUTH CAROLINA

Oklahoma City ★
Little Rock ★

ALABAMA

**Atlanta** ★

Red

MISSISSIPPI

GEORGIA

**Dallas** ■

Jackson ★ Montgomery ★

★ Tallahassee

Baton Rouge ★

**Houston** ■ LOUISIANA

■ **New Orleans**

FLORIDA

ustin ★

an Antonio

● **Miami**

*Gulf of Mexico*

**New York City** The country's
largest city has a magnificent
skyline. It is popularly known
as the 'Big Apple' because it is
a centre of entertainment. It is
also the nation's leading
financial and business centre.

**Baseball** is so popular that
it has been called the
national pastime of the
United States. It was first
played in the mid-18th
century.

**Exploring space** Astronauts
first landed on the moon in a
lunar module like this in 1969.
The United States is now using
probes to explore Mars and the
rest of the solar system.

# Northeastern States

The northeastern states region includes the six New England states of Connecticut, Maine, Massachusetts, New Hampshire, Rhode Island and Vermont. It also includes Delaware, Maryland, New Jersey, New York and Pennsylvania. The map also shows the country's capital, Washington, which lies within an area called the District of Columbia. The Northeast contains fertile farmland, great industrial cities and many historic sites.

**New England** is a historic region that formed part of the original 13 British colonies which became the nucleus for the United States after the Revolutionary War of 1775-83. In the autumn New England's forests are ablaze with colour.

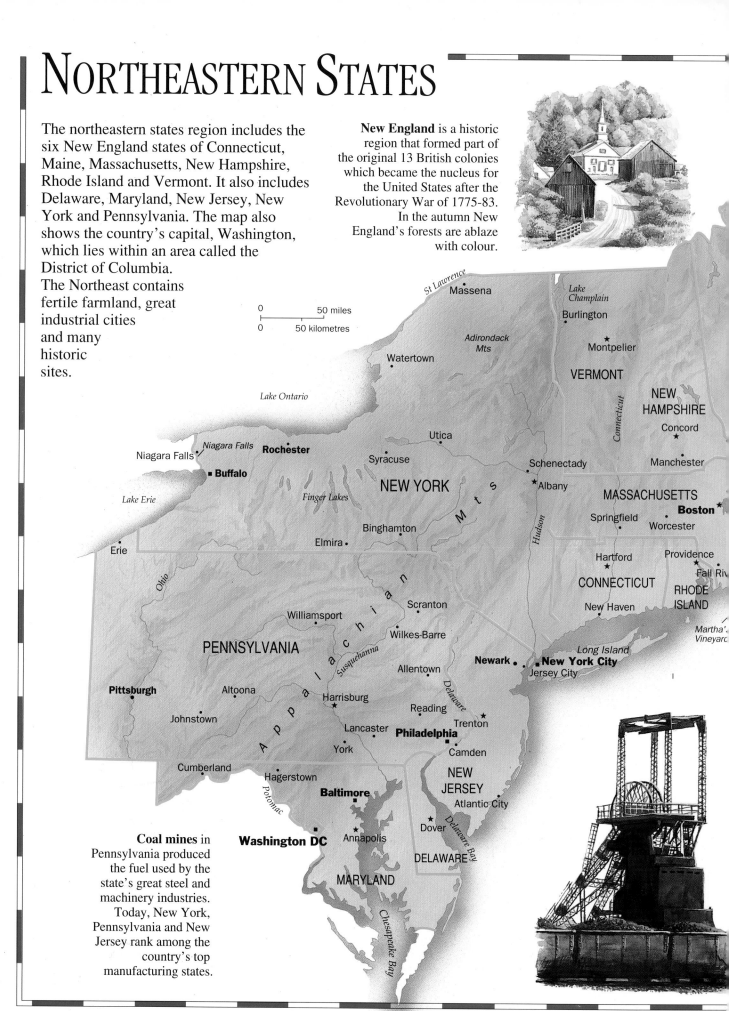

0        50 miles

0        50 kilometres

St Lawrence
Massena
Lake Champlain
Burlington
Adirondack Mts
Montpelier
Watertown
VERMONT
NEW HAMPSHIRE
Concord ★
Lake Ontario
Connecticut
Utica
Niagara Falls
Rochester
Niagara Falls
Syracuse
Schenectady
Manchester
**Buffalo**
NEW YORK
Albany ★
MASSACHUSETTS
Lake Erie
Finger Lakes
Springfield
**Boston** ★
Worcester
Binghamton
Elmira
Erie
Hudson
Hartford ★
Providence ★
Ohio
Fall Riv
CONNECTICUT
RHODE ISLAND
New Haven
Appalachian Mts
Scranton
Martha's Vineyard
Williamsport
Wilkes-Barre
Long Island
PENNSYLVANIA
Susquehanna
Newark ● ■ **New York City**
Jersey City
Allentown
Pittsburgh
Altoona
Harrisburg ★
Reading
Delaware
Trenton ★
Johnstown
Lancaster
Philadelphia ■
York
Camden
Cumberland
NEW JERSEY
Hagerstown
**Baltimore** ■
Atlantic City
Potomac
Dover ★
Delaware Bay
**Washington DC** ■
Annapolis ★
DELAWARE
MARYLAND
Chesapeake Bay

**Coal mines** in Pennsylvania produced the fuel used by the state's great steel and machinery industries. Today, New York, Pennsylvania and New Jersey rank among the country's top manufacturing states.

Presque Isle

Moosehead Lake

MAINE

Bangor

Augusta

rtland

ATLANTIC OCEAN

ape Cod

Nantucket Island

**Capitol** This is the building in Washington DC where Congress (the Senate and the House of Representatives) meets. President George Washington laid its cornerstone in 1793 and Congress first met there in 1800.

**Covered bridges** have a roof and sides that protect the wooden structure from the weather. The first long covered bridge in the United States was built in Massachusetts in 1806.

**Liberty Bell** This church bell in Philadelphia is a symbol of American freedom. It was rung on July 8, 1776, to announce the adoption of the Declaration of Independence. The bell broke in 1835 and is no longer rung.

**Abraham Lincoln** served as president of the United States between 1860 and 1865, when he was assassinated. He led the nation during the Civil War (1861-65).

 **CONNECTICUT**
**Area:** 12,997sq km (5,018sq miles)
**Population:** 3,274,000
**Capital:** Hartford

 **DELAWARE**
**Area:** 5,294sq km (2,045sq miles)
**Population:** 725,000
**Capital:** Dover

 **MAINE**
**Area:** 86,156sq km (33,265sq miles)
**Population:** 1,243,000
**Capital:** Augusta

 **MARYLAND**
**Area:** 27,091sq km (10,460sq miles)
**Population:** 5,072,000
**Capital:** Annapolis

 **MASSACHUSETTS**
**Area:** 21,455sq km (8,284sq miles)
**Population:** 6,092,000
**Capital:** Boston

 **NEW HAMPSHIRE**
**Area:** 24,032sq km (9,279sq miles)
**Population:** 1,162,000
**Capital:** Concord

 **NEW JERSEY**
**Area:** 20,168sq km (7,787sq miles)
**Population:** 7,988,000
**Capital:** Trenton

 **NEW YORK**
**Area:** 136,583sq km (52,735sq miles)
**Population:** 18,185,000
**Capital:** Albany

 **PENNSYLVANIA**
**Area:** 119,251sq km (46,043sq miles)
**Population:** 12,056,000
**Capital:** Harrisburg

 **RHODE ISLAND**
**Area:** 3,139sq km (1,212sq miles)
**Population:** 990,000
**Capital:** Providence

 **VERMONT**
**Area:** 24,900sq km (9,614sq miles)
**Population:** 589,000
**Capital:** Montpelier

**DISTRICT OF COLUMBIA**
**Area:** 179sq km (69sq miles)
**Population:** 543,000

# SOUTHEASTERN STATES

The southeastern states contain large areas of coastal plains and the southern part of the scenic Appalachian Mountains. The region is rich in history. Virginia, North and South Carolina and Georgia were among the 13 English colonies that formed the nucleus of the United States, while the region also played a major part in the Civil War. The states once depended on farming, but manufacturing is now important.

**Coca-Cola** is regarded as a symbol of American taste all over the world. It was first produced by a pharmacist, John S. Pemberton, in Atlanta in 1886. The Coca-Cola Company, founded in 1892, keeps secret the ingredients used in the drink.

**Stone Mountain** This granite mountain near Atlanta, Georgia, has a huge sculpture carved on it as a memorial to the heroes of the South in the Civil War. The sculpture shows Jefferson Davis, Robert E. Lee and Stonewall Jackson.

**Martin Luther King Jr** was the main leader of the Civil Rights movement in the 1950s and 1960s. His demands for justice for African Americans brought him worldwide fame. He was assassinated in 1968.

**American alligators** were once common along the coasts of the Gulf of Mexico and the Atlantic coast as far north as South Carolina. But so many were hunted and killed that they became scarce. Today they are protected in many areas.

**Cotton** was the chief crop of the southeastern states in the 19th century. Before the Civil War, it was picked by slaves. Today the region also produces other warm-weather crops, such as sugar cane, rice and tobacco.

Louisville
Frankfo
★
Lexin
*Ohio*
KENTUCKY
*Cumberland*
★
**Nashville**
Knoxvi
TENNESSEE
• **Memphis**
Chattanooga
*Tennessee*
Birmingham
**Atlar**
ALABAMA
Colum
★
Montgomery
*Alabama*
Mobile
•
• Pensacola
Tallahassee
*Gulf of Mexico*

16

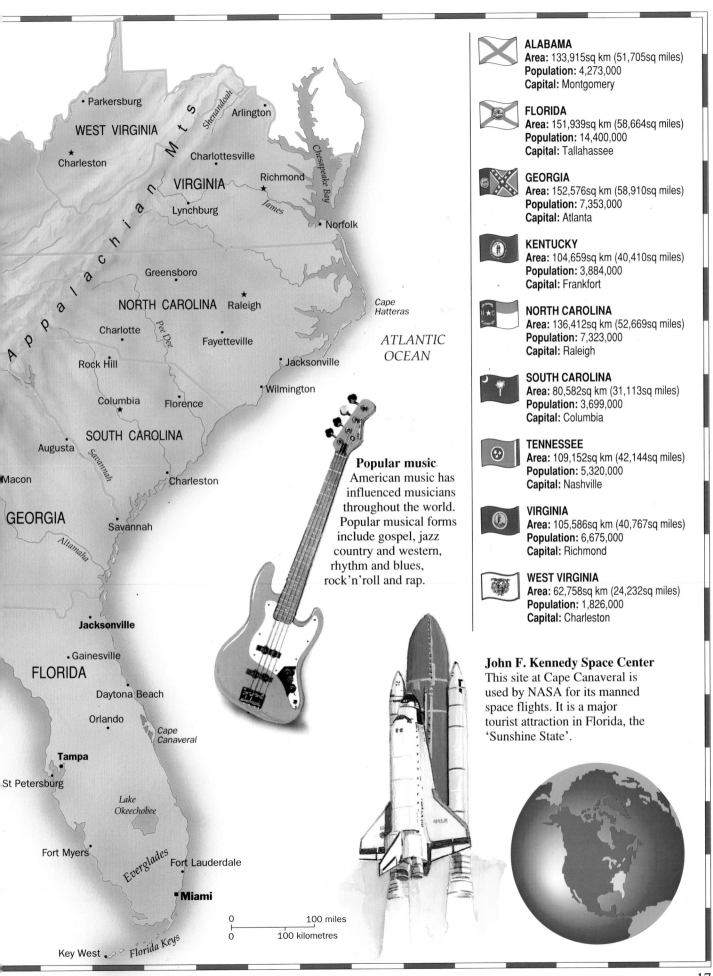

**ALABAMA**
**Area:** 133,915sq km (51,705sq miles)
**Population:** 4,273,000
**Capital:** Montgomery

**FLORIDA**
**Area:** 151,939sq km (58,664sq miles)
**Population:** 14,400,000
**Capital:** Tallahassee

**GEORGIA**
**Area:** 152,576sq km (58,910sq miles)
**Population:** 7,353,000
**Capital:** Atlanta

**KENTUCKY**
**Area:** 104,659sq km (40,410sq miles)
**Population:** 3,884,000
**Capital:** Frankfort

**NORTH CAROLINA**
**Area:** 136,412sq km (52,669sq miles)
**Population:** 7,323,000
**Capital:** Raleigh

**SOUTH CAROLINA**
**Area:** 80,582sq km (31,113sq miles)
**Population:** 3,699,000
**Capital:** Columbia

**TENNESSEE**
**Area:** 109,152sq km (42,144sq miles)
**Population:** 5,320,000
**Capital:** Nashville

**VIRGINIA**
**Area:** 105,586sq km (40,767sq miles)
**Population:** 6,675,000
**Capital:** Richmond

**WEST VIRGINIA**
**Area:** 62,758sq km (24,232sq miles)
**Population:** 1,826,000
**Capital:** Charleston

**Popular music**.
American music has
influenced musicians
throughout the world.
Popular musical forms
include gospel, jazz
country and western,
rhythm and blues,
rock'n'roll and rap.

**John F. Kennedy Space Center**
This site at Cape Canaveral is
used by NASA for its manned
space flights. It is a major
tourist attraction in Florida, the
'Sunshine State'.

ATLANTIC
OCEAN

WEST VIRGINIA
Parkersburg
Charleston ★
Arlington
Charlottesville
VIRGINIA
Richmond ★
Lynchburg
James
Shenandoah
Chesapeake Bay
Norfolk
Appalachian Mts
Greensboro
NORTH CAROLINA   Raleigh ★
Charlotte
Fayetteville
Pee Dee
Rock Hill
Jacksonville
Columbia ★   Florence
Wilmington
Cape Hatteras
SOUTH CAROLINA
Augusta
Savannah
Charleston
Macon
GEORGIA
Savannah
Altamaha
Jacksonville
Gainesville
FLORIDA
Daytona Beach
Orlando
Cape Canaveral
Tampa
St Petersburg
Lake Okeechobee
Fort Myers
Everglades
Fort Lauderdale
Miami
Key West   Florida Keys

0   100 miles
0   100 kilometres

# SOUTH-CENTRAL STATES

Arkansas, Louisiana and Mississippi, which form the eastern part of the south-central states, are drained by the Mississippi River valley. In the west lie the vast open spaces of Texas and Oklahoma. These two states, together with Louisiana, are among the top five petroleum producers in the United States. The region also contains some major cities, including Houston, San Antonio and Dallas, which are among the country's top ten cities.

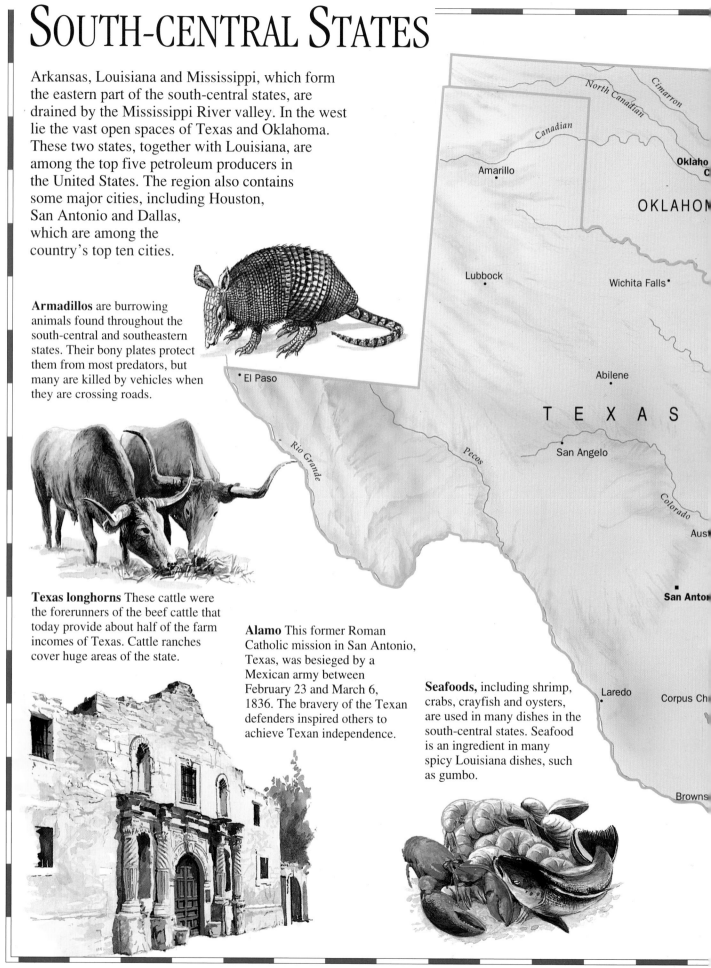

**Armadillos** are burrowing animals found throughout the south-central and southeastern states. Their bony plates protect them from most predators, but many are killed by vehicles when they are crossing roads.

**Texas longhorns** These cattle were the forerunners of the beef cattle that today provide about half of the farm incomes of Texas. Cattle ranches cover huge areas of the state.

**Alamo** This former Roman Catholic mission in San Antonio, Texas, was besieged by a Mexican army between February 23 and March 6, 1836. The bravery of the Texan defenders inspired others to achieve Texan independence.

**Seafoods,** including shrimp, crabs, crayfish and oysters, are used in many dishes in the south-central states. Seafood is an ingredient in many spicy Louisiana dishes, such as gumbo.

Amarillo
Oklaho
C
OKLAHOM
Lubbock
Wichita Falls
El Paso
Abilene
T E X A S
Rio Grande
Pecos
San Angelo
Colorado
Aus
San Anto
Laredo
Corpus Chi
Browns

**ARKANSAS**
**Area:** 137,754sq km (53,187sq miles)
**Population:** 2,510,000
**Capital:** Little Rock

**LOUISIANA**
**Area:** 123,677sq km (47,752sq miles)
**Population:** 4,351,000
**Capital:** Baton Rouge

**MISSISSIPPI**
**Area:** 123,514sq km (47,689sq miles)
**Population:** 2,716,000
**Capital:** Jackson

**OKLAHOMA**
**Area:** 181,185sq km (69,956sq miles)
**Population:** 3,301,000
**Capital:** Oklahoma City

**TEXAS**
**Area:** 691,207sq km (266,807sq miles)
**Population:** 19,128,000
**Capital:** Austin

Tulsa

*Ozark Plateau*

Fort Smith

Little Rock

*Arkansas*

*Ouachita Mts*

ARKANSAS

**Dallas**

t Worth

MISSISSIPPI

aco

Vicksburg

Jackson

Shreveport

*Mississippi*

*Red*

*Pearl*

*Brazos*

LOUISIANA

Baton Rouge

Lafayette

**Houston**

**New Orleans**

Galveston

*Gulf of Mexico*

0        100 miles
0        100 kilometres

**New Orleans**, the largest city in Louisiana, has many old buildings in its fascinating French Quarter. The city was also the birthplace of jazz in the early 20th century.

**Steamboats** still carry passengers along the Mississippi River. This river is the second longest river in the United States after the Missouri. With its tributaries, it drains most of the land between the Appalachians and the Rocky Mountains.

# MIDWESTERN STATES

The 12 Midwestern States cover about a fifth of the United States. The land is mostly flat, including parts of the Great Plains in the west and the lower Interior Plains south and west of the Great Lakes. Farmers produce grains and other crops on the fertile land, together with dairy products and livestock. Major industrial cities include Chicago, Detroit and Indianapolis. The Great Lakes and the Mississippi River are used to transport goods.

**Bison** once roamed the Midwest in huge herds, but hunters slaughtered most of them. Today a few thousand live in protected areas.

**Mount Rushmore National Memorial,** South Dakota, is a carving of four presidents: George Washington, Thomas Jefferson, Theodore Roosevelt and Abraham Lincoln. Each face is about 18m (60ft) high.

**American football** is played by university and college teams. The professional National Football League is divided into the American Football Conference and the National Football Conference.

NORTH DAKOTA
Red Lake
Lake Sakakawea
Fargo • 
Duluth
★ Bismarck
MINNESOTA

Great Plains

Minneapolis • ★ St Paul
SOUTH DAKOTA
Lake Oahe
Mississippi
Black Hills
Pierre ★
▲ Mt Rushmore
Sioux Falls •
Missouri

• Sioux City
Cedar Rapic
IOWA
NEBRASKA
★ Des Moines
Platte
Omaha •
Lincoln ★

Kansas
Kansas City
Topeka ★
Jefferson City
KANSAS
MISSOUR
Wichita

**Pioneers** had reached the Mississippi by the 1820s. In the 1840s wagon trains crossed the Great Plains and, by the 1890s, scattered settlements had sprung up all across this dry region.

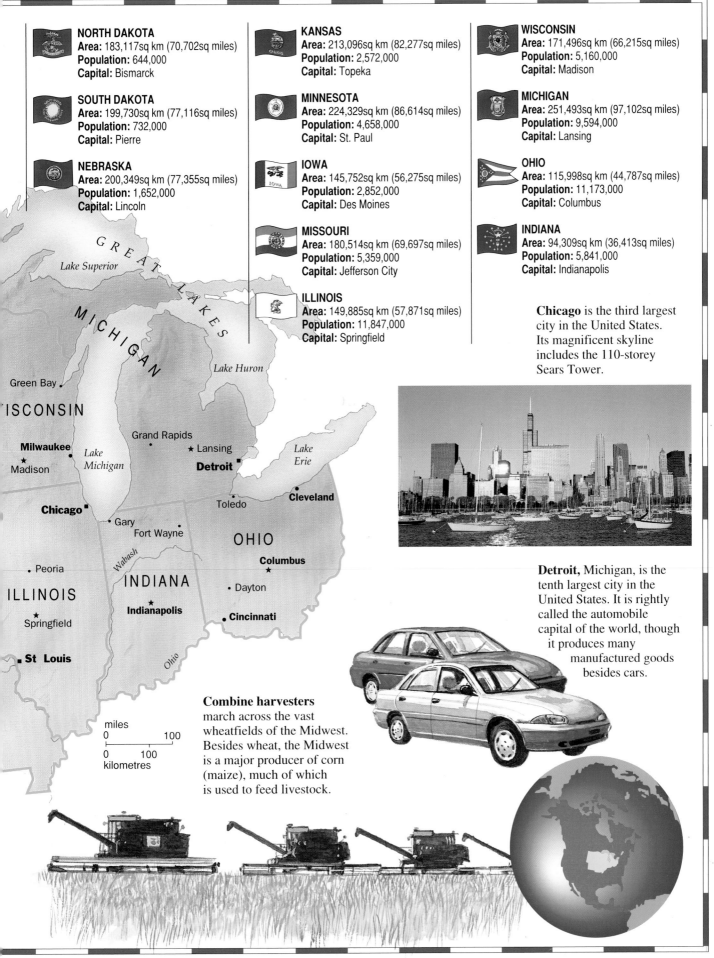

**NORTH DAKOTA**
**Area:** 183,117sq km (70,702sq miles)
**Population:** 644,000
**Capital:** Bismarck

**SOUTH DAKOTA**
**Area:** 199,730sq km (77,116sq miles)
**Population:** 732,000
**Capital:** Pierre

**NEBRASKA**
**Area:** 200,349sq km (77,355sq miles)
**Population:** 1,652,000
**Capital:** Lincoln

**KANSAS**
**Area:** 213,096sq km (82,277sq miles)
**Population:** 2,572,000
**Capital:** Topeka

**MINNESOTA**
**Area:** 224,329sq km (86,614sq miles)
**Population:** 4,658,000
**Capital:** St. Paul

**IOWA**
**Area:** 145,752sq km (56,275sq miles)
**Population:** 2,852,000
**Capital:** Des Moines

**MISSOURI**
**Area:** 180,514sq km (69,697sq miles)
**Population:** 5,359,000
**Capital:** Jefferson City

**ILLINOIS**
**Area:** 149,885sq km (57,871sq miles)
**Population:** 11,847,000
**Capital:** Springfield

**WISCONSIN**
**Area:** 171,496sq km (66,215sq miles)
**Population:** 5,160,000
**Capital:** Madison

**MICHIGAN**
**Area:** 251,493sq km (97,102sq miles)
**Population:** 9,594,000
**Capital:** Lansing

**OHIO**
**Area:** 115,998sq km (44,787sq miles)
**Population:** 11,173,000
**Capital:** Columbus

**INDIANA**
**Area:** 94,309sq km (36,413sq miles)
**Population:** 5,841,000
**Capital:** Indianapolis

GREAT LAKES

MICHIGAN

Lake Superior

Lake Huron

Green Bay

WISCONSIN

Milwaukee

Madison

Lake Michigan

Grand Rapids

★ Lansing

**Detroit**

Lake Erie

**Cleveland**

Toledo

**Chicago**

Gary

Fort Wayne

OHIO

Wabash

**Columbus**
★

Peoria

INDIANA

Dayton

ILLINOIS

**Indianapolis**
★

**Cincinnati**

Springfield
★

St Louis

Ohio

miles
0 — 100
0 — 100
kilometres

**Chicago** is the third largest city in the United States. Its magnificent skyline includes the 110-storey Sears Tower.

**Detroit,** Michigan, is the tenth largest city in the United States. It is rightly called the automobile capital of the world, though it produces many manufactured goods besides cars.

**Combine harvesters** march across the vast wheatfields of the Midwest. Besides wheat, the Midwest is a major producer of corn (maize), much of which is used to feed livestock.

# NORTHWESTERN STATES

The eastern part of the northwestern states is part of the flat Great Plains. But the west is largely mountainous. The Cascade Range in Oregon and Washington has active volcanoes, including Mount Saint Helens, which exploded with great force in 1980, killing 57 people. Alaska, which became the 49th state on 3 January 1959, also has active volcanoes. Alaska is rich in oil, while farming and forestry are important in the other five states.

**Aircraft** Commercial and military aircraft as well as other military hardware are made by the Boeing Company, which has its headquarters in Seattle, Washington. The manufacture of wood products and processed foods are other major industries in the Northwest.

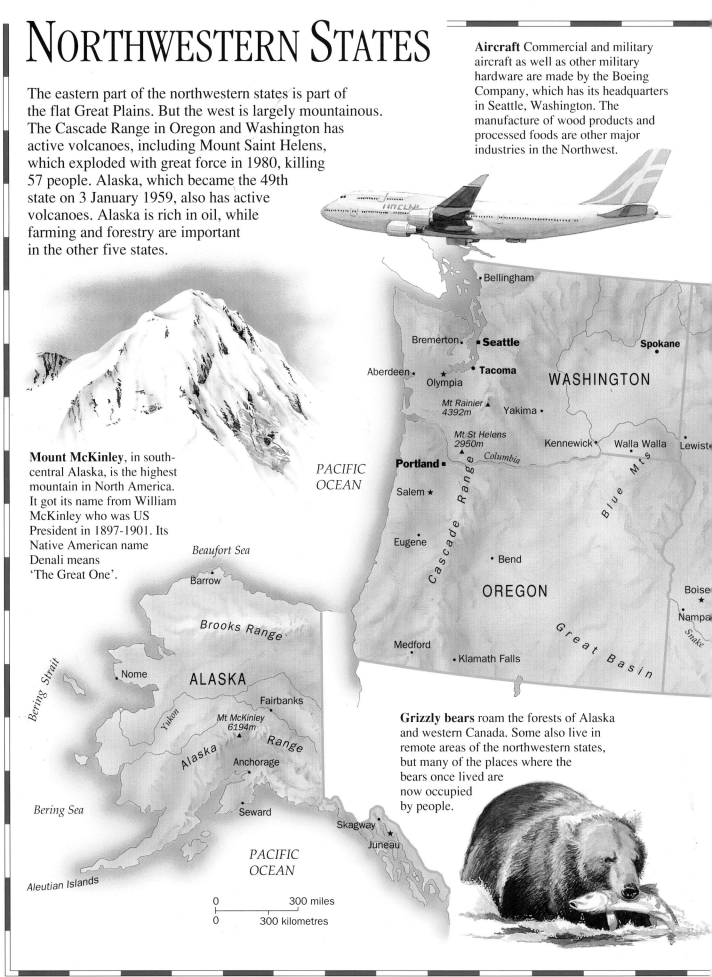

**Mount McKinley**, in south-central Alaska, is the highest mountain in North America. It got its name from William McKinley who was US President in 1897-1901. Its Native American name Denali means 'The Great One'.

*PACIFIC OCEAN*

**Grizzly bears** roam the forests of Alaska and western Canada. Some also live in remote areas of the northwestern states, but many of the places where the bears once lived are now occupied by people.

Bellingham

Bremerton · · **Seattle**    **Spokane** ·

Aberdeen ·    · **Tacoma**
Olympia ★    WASHINGTON

Mt Rainier ▲    · Yakima
4392m

Mt St Helens    Kennewick ·   · Walla Walla    Lewist
2950m
▲    *Columbia*

**Portland** ■    Cascade Range

Salem ★    Blue Mts

Eugene    · Bend

OREGON    Boise
★
· Nampa

Medford ·    G r e a t    *Snake*
· Klamath Falls    B a s i n

*Beaufort Sea*

Barrow

Brooks Range

*Bering Strait*    Nome ·    ALASKA

*Yukon*    Fairbanks ·

Mt McKinley    Range
6194m
▲

Alaska    Anchorage

*Bering Sea*    Seward ·

Skagway ·
★
Juneau

*PACIFIC OCEAN*

*Aleutian Islands*

| 0 | | 300 miles |
|---|---|---|
| 0 | | 300 kilometres |

**ALASKA**
**Area:** 1,530,693sq km
(591,004sq miles)
**Population:** 607,000
**Capital:** Juneau

 **IDAHO**
**Area:** 216,430sq km (83,564sq miles)
**Population:** 1,189,000
**Capital:** Boise

 **MONTANA**
**Area:** 380,849sq km (147,046sq miles)
**Population:** 879,000
**Capital:** Helena

 **OREGON**
**Area:** 251,418sq km (97,073sq miles)
**Population:** 3,204,000
**Capital:** Salem

 **WASHINGTON**
**Area:** 176,479sq km (68,139sq miles)
**Population:** 5,553,000
**Capital:** Olympia

 **WYOMING**
**Area:** 253,324sq km (97,809sq miles)
**Population:** 481,000
**Capital:** Cheyenne

**Native Americans** in the Northwest fished and hunted animals. They also gathered plant foods in the forests. They used wood to build houses and boats, and to make containers, bowls, utensils and masks like this one.

**Yellowstone National Park** lies mainly in northwestern Wyoming. It was set up in 1872 and is the world's oldest national park. It contains hot springs and geysers, canyons and huge waterfalls.

0         100 miles

0         100 kilometres

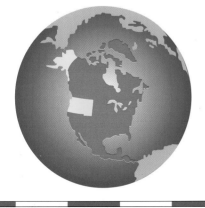

**Devils Tower**, in northeastern Wyoming, is a mountain formed from hard volcanic rock. It rises 264m (865ft) from its base. It became the country's first national monument in 1906.

# SOUTHWESTERN STATES

The southwestern states contain much magnificent scenery. California has more people than any other state and is the country's leading manufacturing and farming state. It also has valuable mineral deposits, including oil and natural gas. If California were a separate country, it would rank among the world's top ten in terms of the total value of the goods and services it produces. Hawaii, in the Pacific Ocean, became the 50th state on 21 August 1959.

**Surfing** is an exciting sport along the Pacific coast of California and also in Hawaii. The northern shores of Oahu, Hawaii, attract surfers from all over the world.

**Silicon Valley** is an area in California between San Jose and nearby Palo Alto that is home to the computer industry. Silicon is used to make the microprocessors in computers.

**Deserts** cover large areas in the Southwest. Some desert plants, such as cacti, have long, shallow roots that obtain every drop of moisture from a large area. Their swollen stems store water.

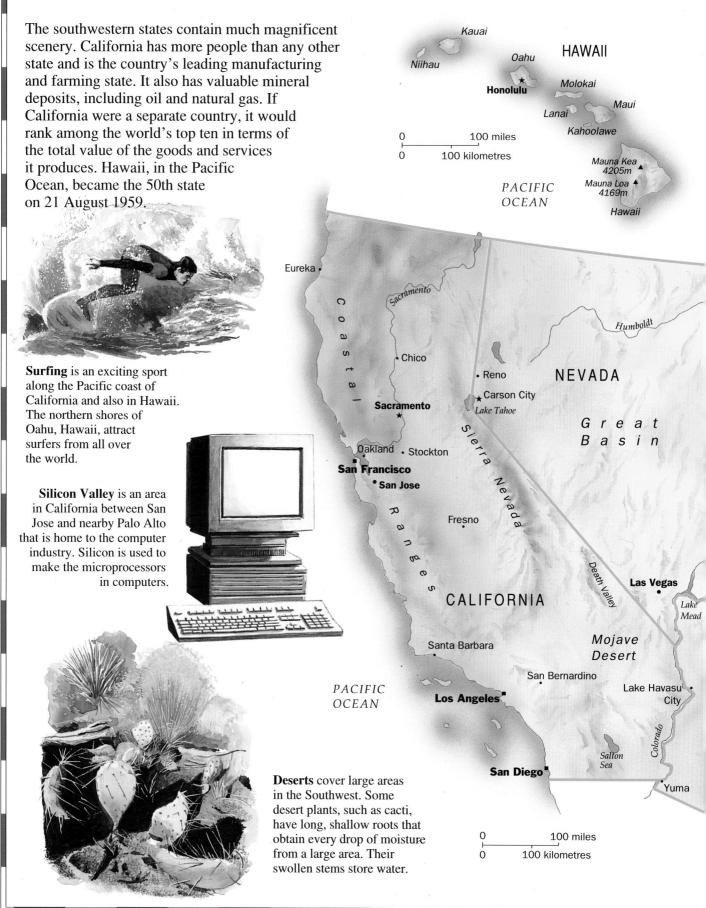

HAWAII

Kauai
Niihau
Oahu
★ Honolulu
Molokai
Lanai
Maui
Kahoolawe

0 — 100 miles
0 — 100 kilometres

Mauna Kea 4205m ▲
Mauna Loa 4169m ▲
Hawaii

PACIFIC OCEAN

Eureka •

Coastal

Sacramento

• Chico

• Reno

NEVADA

Humboldt

★ Carson City
Lake Tahoe

Sacramento ★

Oakland • Stockton
San Francisco
• San Jose

Sierra Nevada

Great Basin

Ranges

Fresno •

Death Valley

Las Vegas •

Lake Mead

CALIFORNIA

Santa Barbara •

Mojave Desert

San Bernardino •

Lake Havasu City

PACIFIC OCEAN

Los Angeles •

Colorado

Salton Sea

San Diego •

Yuma •

0 — 100 miles
0 — 100 kilometres

**Kilauea** is an active volcano on the eastern slope of Mauna Loa, Hawaii. It emits runny lava that flows down to the sea. All of the islands in Hawaii were formed by volcanoes. But only the volcanoes on Hawaii itself are active. The others are extinct.

**Grand Canyon** This huge canyon was worn out by the Colorado River and is around 1.6km (1mile) deep in places. The canyon, like many of the country's scenic wonders, is protected in a national park.

 **ARIZONA**
**Area:** 295,259sq km (114,000sq miles)
**Population:** 4,428,000
**Capital:** Phoenix

 **CALIFORNIA**
**Area:** 411,047sq km (158,706sq miles)
**Population:** 31,878,000
**Capital:** Sacramento

 **COLORADO**
**Area:** 269,594sq km (104,091sq miles)
**Population:** 3,823,000
**Capital:** Denver

 **HAWAII**
**Area:** 16,760sq km (6,471sq miles)
**Population:** 1,184,000
**Capital:** Honolulu

 **NEVADA**
**Area:** 286,352sq km (110,561sq miles)
**Population:** 1,603,000
**Capital:** Carson City

 **NEW MEXICO**
**Area:** 314,924sq km (121,593sq miles)
**Population:** 1,713,000
**Capital:** Santa Fe

 **UTAH**
**Area:** 219,887sq km (84,899sq miles)
**Population:** 2,000,000
**Capital:** Salt Lake City

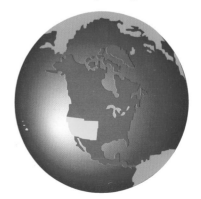

**Mesa Verde** is a national park in southwestern Colorado. Its name means 'green table' and it contains impressive remains of cliff dwellings built by Native Americans hundreds of years ago.

# MEXICO

Mexico, the third largest country in North America, forms a bridge between the United States and the seven countries of Central America. The land is mainly mountainous, with deserts in the north and rainforests in the south. Temperatures vary according to the height of the land. Farming is important, but Mexico's main exports are oil and oil products. Factories in the north assemble goods, such as vehicle parts, for US companies.

**MEXICO**

**Area:** 1,972,547sq km (761,605sq miles)
**Highest point:** Citlaltépetl (also called Orizaba), 5,700m (18,701ft)
**Population:** 93,182,000
**Capital:** Mexico City (pop 15,643,000)
**Other large cities:** Guadalajara (2,847,000) Monterrey (2,522,000) Puebla (1,055,000)
**Official language:** Spanish
**Religions:** Roman Catholic 90%, Protestant 5%, others 5%
**Government:** Federal republic
**Currency:** Mexican peso

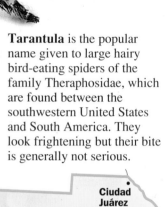

**Tarantula** is the popular name given to large hairy bird-eating spiders of the family Theraphosidae, which are found between the southwestern United States and South America. They look frightening but their bite is generally not serious.

**Monarch butterfly** This colourful creature holds the record among insects for the distance it migrates each year. In autumn, it travels from New England to the southern United States and Mexico. In spring it returns to the north.

**Acapulco** is Mexico's leading Pacific Ocean resort. Tourism is a major industry in Mexico. Some people come to the seaside resorts while others want to see the great Native American historic sites.

**Gold and silver** objects made by Aztecs are evidence of their artistic skills. According to legend, the Aztec capital, Tenochtitlán, was founded in 1325. The Aztecs were defeated by Spanish soldiers in 1521.

Tijuana  Mexicali  *Colorado*

Ciudad Juárez

Hermosillo

Chihuahua

*Baja California*

*Gulf of California*

*Sierra Madre Occidental*

Culiacán

La Paz

Dura

Mazatlán

PACIFIC OCEAN

Te

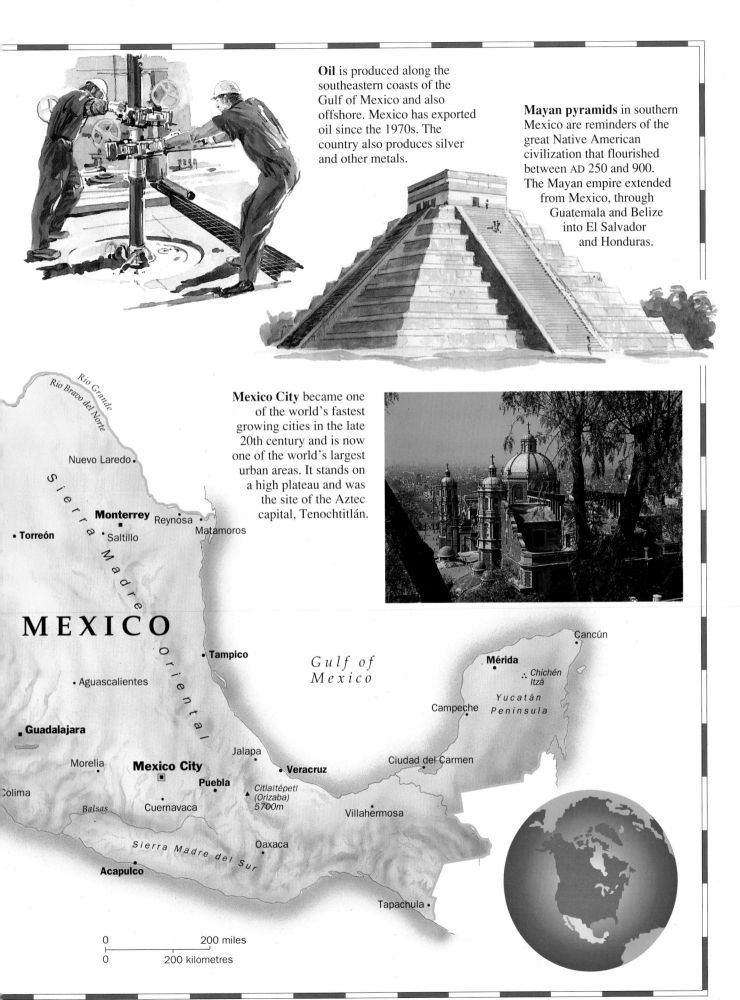

**Oil** is produced along the southeastern coasts of the Gulf of Mexico and also offshore. Mexico has exported oil since the 1970s. The country also produces silver and other metals.

**Mayan pyramids** in southern Mexico are reminders of the great Native American civilization that flourished between AD 250 and 900. The Mayan empire extended from Mexico, through Guatemala and Belize into El Salvador and Honduras.

**Mexico City** became one of the world's fastest growing cities in the late 20th century and is now one of the world's largest urban areas. It stands on a high plateau and was the site of the Aztec capital, Tenochtitlán.

Rio Grande
Rio Bravo del Norte

Nuevo Laredo •

Sierra Madre Oriental

**Monterrey** ■   Reynosa •

• **Torreón**    • Saltillo    Matamoros •

**MEXICO**

• Aguascalientes

• **Tampico**

*Gulf of Mexico*

Cancún

**Mérida** •    •. *Chichén Itzá*

*Yucatán Peninsula*

Campeche •

**Guadalajara** ■

Morelia •    **Mexico City** ▣    **Puebla** •    *Citlaltépetl (Orizaba) 5700m* ▲    • **Veracruz**    Jalapa •

Ciudad del Carmen

Colima    *Balsas*    Cuernavaca    Villahermosa •

Oaxaca •

*Sierra Madre del Sur*

**Acapulco** •

Tapachula •

| 0 | | 200 miles |
|---|---|---|
| 0 | | 200 kilometres |

27

# WESTERN CENTRAL AMERICA

Western Central America consists of four countries: Belize, El Salvador, Guatemala and Honduras. Hot and humid coasts border the region in the north and south. Between lies a highland zone with many active volcanoes. The people include Native Americans, together with people of African and European descent. Many people are of mixed origin. Farming is the main activity. Most people live in the cooler highlands.

**Coral reefs and islands** stretch along the swampy coast of Belize. They form the world's second longest barrier reef after Australia's Great Barrier Reef and they are an important breeding area for fish.

## BELIZE

**Area:** 22,965sq km (8,867sq miles)
**Population:** 222,000
**Capital:** Belmopan (pop 5,000)
**Largest city:** Belize City (48,000)
**Government:** Constitutional monarchy
**Official language:** English
**Currency:** Belize dollar

## EL SALVADOR

**Area:** 21,041sq km (8,124 sq miles)
**Population:** 5,810,000
**Capital and largest city:** San Salvador (pop 1,522,000)
**Government:** Republic
**Official language:** Spanish
**Currency:** Colón

## GUATEMALA

**Area:** 108,889sq km (42,042sq miles)
**Population:** 10,928,000
**Capital and largest city:** Guatemala City (pop. 2,000,000)
**Government:** Republic
**Official language:** Spanish
**Currency:** Quetzal

## HONDURAS

**Area:** 112,088sq km (43,277sq miles)
**Population:** 6,101,000
**Capital and largest city:** Tegucigalpa (pop 679,000)
**Government:** Republic
**Official language:** Spanish
**Currency:** Lempira

0 ___ 50 miles
0 ___ 50 kilometres

Belize Cit
Tikal
Belmopan
**BELIZE**
Chixoy
Puerto Barrios
**GUATEMALA**
Lake Izabal
▲ Tajumulco 4210m
Quezaltenango
Motagua
Mazatenango
**Guatemala City**
Antigua
*PACIFIC OCEAN*
Santa Ana
San **Salvador**
Sonsonate
**EL SALVADOR**

**Coffee** is grown in the highlands of Central America and most of the berries on the coffee plants are hand picked. Coffee is the chief export of El Salvador, Guatemala and Honduras.

**Tikal,** in northern Guatemala, contains huge ruined pyramids. It was the biggest city of the Maya. Its main temple stood on top of a pyramid 45 metres (150ft) tall.

**Bananas** grow well in hot, wet climates and they are a leading crop on the lowlands of Central America. The other main crop grown for export in lowland areas is sugar cane.

*Caribbean Sea*

*Gulf of Honduras*

*Islas de la Bahia*

Tela

La Ceiba

an Pedro
Sula

*Patuca*

Juticalpa

# HONDURAS

Tegucigalpa

Miguel

**Manatees,** or sea cows, live along the Caribbean coasts of Central America and northern South America. Found in sheltered coastal waters, they have suffered from the effects of pollution and the use of power boats.

**Market days** in Guatemalan towns and villages are lively occasions, when farmers bring their products for sale. About 45 per cent of Guatemala's people are direct descendants of the original Native Americans.

# EASTERN CENTRAL AMERICA

Like western Central America, Costa Rica, Nicaragua and Panama have hot, tropical climates except in highland areas which are cooler. Nicaragua is the largest country in Central America. Like Costa Rica, it lies in an unstable area where earthquakes and volcanic eruptions are common. Costa Rica has many beautiful national parks and now attracts many tourists. Panama is an isthmus, a narrow strip of land linking North and South America.

## COSTA RICA

**Area:** 50,700sq km (19,575sq miles)
**Population:** 3,442,000
**Capital:** San José
**Largest city:** San José (1,186,000)
**Government:** Republic
**Official language:** Spanish
**Religions:** Christianity (Roman Catholic 80%)
**Currency:** Costa Rican colón

## NICARAGUA

**Area:** 130,000sq km (50,193sq miles)
**Population:** 6,101,000
**Capital:** Managua
**Largest city:** Managua (974,000)
**Government:** Republic
**Official language:** Spanish
**Religions:** Christianity (Roman Catholic 77%)
**Currency:** Córdoba

## PANAMA

**Area:** 77,082sq km (29,762sq miles)
**Population:** 2,674,000
**Capital:** Panama City
**Largest city:** Panama City (452,000)
**Government:** Republic
**Official language:** Spanish
**Religions:** Christianity (Roman Catholic 80%)
**Currency:** Balboa

**Pan-American Highway**
This road system extends through the Americas from the United States border to southern Chile. The only break is in Panama where the route is blocked by dense rainforest.

**Active volcanoes** Volcanic eruptions are common throughout the highlands of Nicaragua and Costa Rica. The volcanic rocks have weathered to produce rich, fertile soils.

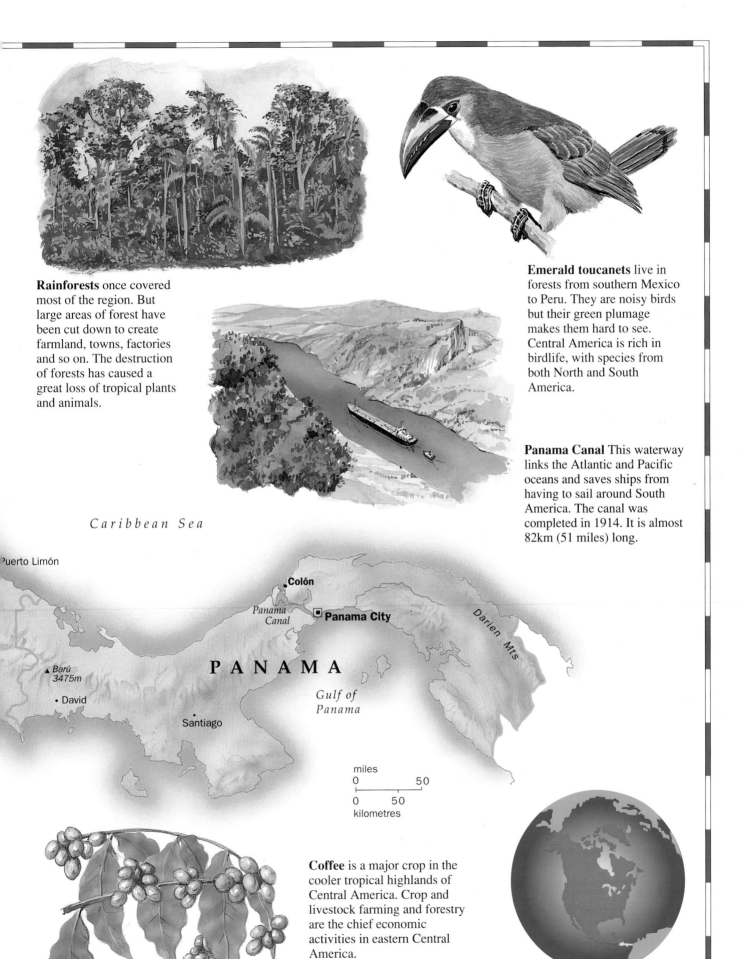

**Rainforests** once covered most of the region. But large areas of forest have been cut down to create farmland, towns, factories and so on. The destruction of forests has caused a great loss of tropical plants and animals.

**Emerald toucanets** live in forests from southern Mexico to Peru. They are noisy birds but their green plumage makes them hard to see. Central America is rich in birdlife, with species from both North and South America.

**Panama Canal** This waterway links the Atlantic and Pacific oceans and saves ships from having to sail around South America. The canal was completed in 1914. It is almost 82km (51 miles) long.

*Caribbean Sea*

Puerto Limón

•**Colón**

*Panama Canal*

□ **Panama City**

*Darien Mts*

**P A N A M A**

▲ *Barú 3475m*

• David

*Gulf of Panama*

• Santiago

miles
0          50
|----------|
0     50
kilometres

**Coffee** is a major crop in the cooler tropical highlands of Central America. Crop and livestock farming and forestry are the chief economic activities in eastern Central America.

31

# NORTHERN CARIBBEAN

The largest Caribbean island nations are Cuba, the Dominican Republic and Haiti, followed by the Bahamas and Jamaica. Puerto Rico is a US Commonwealth, while the Cayman Islands and the Turks and Caicos Islands are British overseas territories. Most people are descended from Europeans, and Africans who came to the Caribbean as slaves. Sugar and coffee are leading crops. Manufacturing, mining and tourism are also important.

**Fidel Castro** led revolutionary forces to power in Cuba in 1959. His Communist policies and his close ties with the former Soviet Union were opposed by the United States.

## BAHAMAS

**Area:** 13,935sq km (5,380sq miles)
**Population:** 284,000
**Capital:** Nassau (pop 172,000)
**Currency:** Bahamian dollar

## CUBA

**Area:** 110,861sq km (42,804sq miles)
**Population:** 11,019,000
**Capital:** Havana (pop 2,096,000)
**Currency:** Cuban peso

## DOMINICAN REPUBLIC

**Area:** 48,734sq km (18,816sq miles)
**Population:** 7,964,000
**Capital:** Santo Domingo (pop 1,601,000)
**Currency:** Dominican peso

## HAITI

**Area:** 27,750sq km (10,714sq miles)
**Population:** 7,336,000
**Capital:** Port-au-Prince (pop 1,144,000)
**Currency:** Gourde

## JAMAICA

**Area:** 10,991sq km (4,244sq miles)
**Population:** 2,547,000
**Capital:** Kingston (pop 588,000)
**Currency:** Jamaican dollar

## OVERSEAS TERRITORIES

**CAYMAN ISLANDS (UK)**
**Area:** 259sq km (100sq miles)
**Population:** 32,000
**Capital:** George Town

**PUERTO RICO (US)**
**Area:** 8,897sq km (3,435sq miles)
**Population:** 3,783,000
**Capital:** San Juan

**TURKS AND CAICOS ISLANDS (UK)**
**Area:** 430sq km (166sq miles)
**Population:** 15,000
**Capital:** Cockburn Town

Little Abaco

Grand Bahama

Great Abaco

New Providenc

**Nassa**

Andros

Gulf of Mexico   **Havana**   **Matanzas**

BAHAMA

Pinar del Rio

Santa Clara

**Cienfuegos**   Sancti Spiritus   **Morón**

Ciego de Avila

Isle of Youth

CUBA   **Camagüey**

Bay

George Town

CAYMAN ISLANDS (UK)

Montego Bay

**Kings**

Spanish Tow

JAMAIC

Caribbean Sea

**Cricket** is a major sport in Jamaica. It was introduced by the British, who ruled the island for about 300 years until it became independent in 1962. The official language in Jamaica is English.

**Sugar cane** is grown in many Caribbean islands and it is Cuba's leading export. The islands also produce minerals, including nickel (Cuba), iron and nickel (Dominican Republic) and bauxite (Jamaica).

**Banking** and other financial services are important in the Bahamas. Many foreign firms and banks have branches there. The islands have no direct taxes and so many people invest money in the banks.

**Tourism** is a major activity in the Caribbean. Swimming and snorkelling in the sparkling, sunlit water around the islands in the Bahamas are popular sports. More than 1.5 million tourists visit the Bahamas every year.

**San Juan** is the capital and largest city of Puerto Rico, a self-governing commonwealth in association with the United States. The chief jobs of the people are in manufacturing, trade and government.

Eleuthera

Cat

San Salvador

Rum Cay

Great Exuma

Long

Crooked

Mayaguana

Acklins

Great Inagua

• Cockburn Town

**TURKS AND CAICOS ISLANDS (UK)**

*ATLANTIC OCEAN*

• **Holguin**

**Guantánamo**

**Santiago de Cuba**

Cap-Haïtien

Santiago

San Francisco

Gonaives •

**HAITI**

**DOMINICAN REPUBLIC**

**Port-au-Prince**

La Romana

**PUERTO RICO (US)**

**San Juan**

**Santo Domingo**

Les Cayes

Jacmel

Ponce

0 ⊢──────────⊣ 100 miles
0 ⊢──────────⊣ 100 kilometres

**Roman Catholicism** was introduced into Cuba and the Dominican Republic by Spain, and into Haiti by France. But Protestantism is important in Jamaica and the Bahamas, which were influenced by Britain.

# EASTERN CARIBBEAN

The eastern Caribbean consists mostly of small islands. Some are volcanic, while others are made of coral and limestone. The region contains eight independent countries and eight territories linked to France, the Netherlands, the United States and the UK. Farming and tourism are the chief activities, though Trinidad and Tobago has oil and natural gas. Native Americans once lived on the islands, but people of African descent now form the majority.

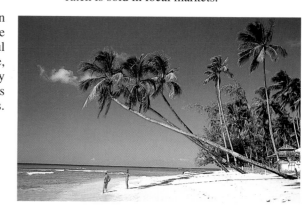

(UK)
Road Tow
Charlotte Amalie
**VIRGIN ISLAND**
(US)

**Dolphins** of several species live in the waters of the Caribbean Sea. Tourists on cruise ships enjoy watching the dolphins. Fishing is an important industry, but nearly all of the catch is sold in local markets.

*Coconut*

*Sugar cane*

*Mace*

*Cloves*

*Nutmeg*

*Cinnamon*

**Tourism** is a major industry in the eastern Caribbean.The islands are scenically beautiful and have many attractive, sun-baked beaches. Many people visit the islands on cruise ships.

**Spices**, such as cinnamon and nutmeg, are grown on some of the islands in the eastern Caribbean. The main products of the islands include bananas, coconuts, cotton and sugar.

**Massive eruptions** of the Soufrière Hills volcano, on Montserrat, forced many people to leave their homes or leave the island in the late 1990s. The capital Plymouth was covered by volcanic ash.

**ARUBA (Neth)**       **NETHERLANDS ANTILLES**

*Aruba*          *Curaçao*
                          *Bonaire*
              Willemstad

0                    100 miles

0          100 kilometres

SOUTH  AMERICA

**Sailing and fishing** are popular tourist activities in the blue waters of the eastern Caribbean. Local people enjoy a variety of sports, including basketball, cricket and soccer.

**ANGUILLA (UK)**
The Valley

*ATLANTIC OCEAN*

**ANTIGUA AND BARBUDA**
Saint John's

**ST KITTS AND NEVIS**
Basseterre

Plymouth
**MONTSERRAT (UK)**

**GUADELOUPE (Fr)**
Basse Terre

**DOMINICA**
Roseau

Fort-de-France
**MARTINIQUE ( Fr)**

*Caribbean Sea*

Castries
**ST LUCIA**

**ST VINCENT AND THE GRENADINES**
Kingstown

Bridgetown
**BARBADOS**

**GRENADA**
Saint George's

Tobago

**TRINIDAD AND TOBAGO**
Port of Spain

*Trinidad*

## OVERSEAS TERRITORIES

**ANGUILLA (UK)**
**Area:** 96sq km (37sq miles)
**Population:** 8,000
**Capital:** The Valley

**ARUBA (NETHERLANDS)**
**Area:** 75sq km (29sq miles)
**Population:** 77,000
**Capital:** Oranjestad

**GUADELOUPE (FRANCE)**
**Area:** 1,705sq km (658sq miles)
**Population:** 422,000
**Capital:** Basse Terre

**MARTINIQUE (FRANCE)**
**Area:** 1,102sq km (425sq miles)
**Population:** 384,000
**Capital:** Fort-de-France

**MONTSERRAT (UK)**
**Area:** 102sq km (39sq miles)
**Population:** 11,000
**Capital:** Plymouth

**NETHERLANDS ANTILLES**
**Area:** 800sq km (309sq miles)
**Population:** 202,000
**Capital:** Willemstad

**VIRGIN ISLANDS (US)**
**Area:** 340sq km (131sq miles)
**Population:** 98,000
**Capital:** Charlotte Amalie

**VIRGIN ISLANDS (UK)**
**Area:** 153sq km (59sq miles)
**Population:** 20,000
**Capital:** Road Town

## ANTIGUA AND BARBUDA

**Area:** 440sq km (170sq miles)
**Population:** 66,000
**Capital:** Saint John's (pop 38,000)
**Currency:** East Caribbean dollar

## BARBADOS

**Area:** 431sq km (166sq miles)
**Population:** 264,000
**Capital:** Bridgetown (pop 8,000)
**Currency:** Barbados dollar

## DOMINICA

**Area:** 751sq km (290sq miles)
**Population:** 74,000
**Capital:** Roseau (pop 21,000)
**Currency:** East Caribbean dollar

## GRENADA

**Area:** 344sq km (133sq miles)
**Population:** 99,000
**Capital:** St. George's (pop 7,000)
**Currency:** East Caribbean dollar

## ST KITTS AND NEVIS

**Area:** 261sq km (101sq miles)
**Population:** 41,000
**Capital:** Basseterre (pop 15,000)
**Currency:** East Caribbean dollar

## ST LUCIA

**Area:** 616sq km (238sq miles)
**Population:** 158,000
**Capital:** Castries (pop 54,000)
**Currency:** East Caribbean dollar

## ST VINCENT AND THE GRENADINES

**Area:** 388sq km (150sq miles)
**Population:** 112,000
**Capital:** Kingstown (pop 27,000)
**Currency:** East Caribbean dollar

## TRINIDAD AND TOBAGO

**Area:** 5,130sq km (1,981sq miles)
**Population:** 1,297,000
**Capital:** Port of Spain (pop 46,000)
**Currency:** Trinidad & Tobago dollar

# PEOPLE AND BELIEFS

North America contains eight per cent of the world's population. Vast areas, including most of Canada and Alaska and the deserts of the southwestern United States and northern Mexico, are almost empty of people. Thickly populated areas, with many huge cities, occur in the eastern United States, California, the Mexican plateau, Central America and the Caribbean.

**Population densities in North America**

Number of people per square kilometre

- Over 100
- Between 50 and 100
- Between 10 and 50
- Between 1 and 10
- Below 1

**The main cities**

- ■ Cities of more than 1,000,000 people
- ● Cities of more than 500,000 people

## Population and area

Although Canada is the world's second largest country, its population of over 30 million is only about one-ninth that of the United States and one-third that of Mexico. Around 200 years ago, more than 90 per cent of North Americans lived in rural areas and farmed the land. Today 65 per cent live in towns and cities, including Mexico City, the world's largest, New York City, Los Angeles and Chicago.

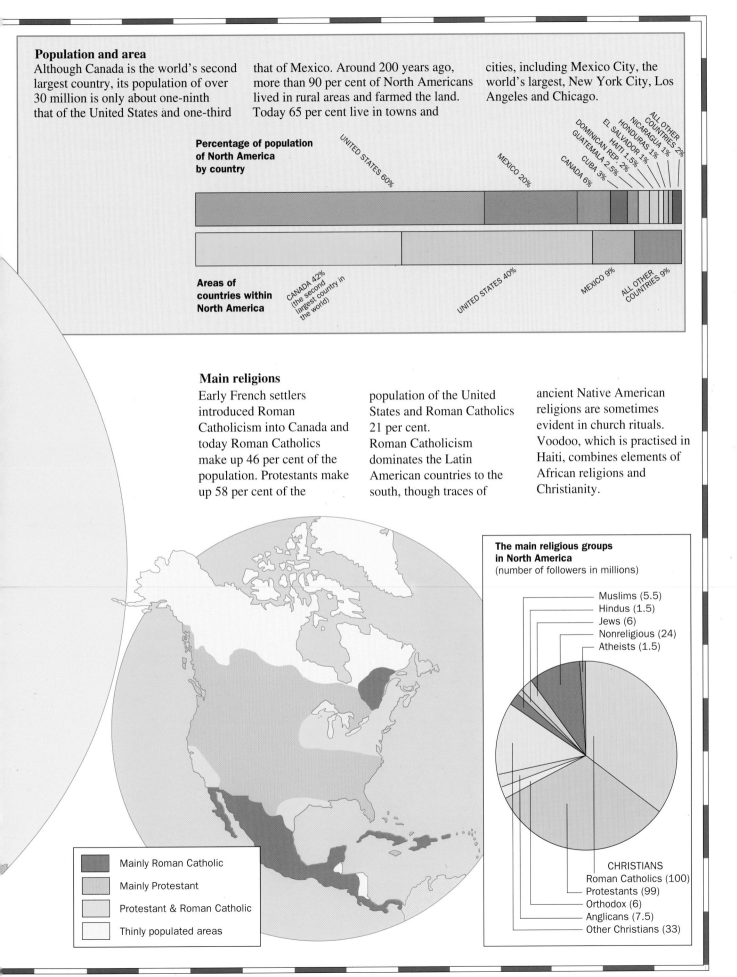

Percentage of population of North America by country

UNITED STATES 60%
MEXICO 20%
CANADA 6%
CUBA 3%
GUATEMALA 2.5%
DOMINICAN REP. 2%
EL SALVADOR 1.5%
HAITI 1.5%
HONDURAS 1%
NICARAGUA 1%
ALL OTHER COUNTRIES 2%

Areas of countries within North America

CANADA 42% (the second largest country in the world)
UNITED STATES 40%
MEXICO 9%
ALL OTHER COUNTRIES 9%

## Main religions

Early French settlers introduced Roman Catholicism into Canada and today Roman Catholics make up 46 per cent of the population. Protestants make up 58 per cent of the population of the United States and Roman Catholics 21 per cent. Roman Catholicism dominates the Latin American countries to the south, though traces of ancient Native American religions are sometimes evident in church rituals. Voodoo, which is practised in Haiti, combines elements of African religions and Christianity.

**The main religious groups in North America**
(number of followers in millions)

Muslims (5.5)
Hindus (1.5)
Jews (6)
Nonreligious (24)
Atheists (1.5)

CHRISTIANS
Roman Catholics (100)
Protestants (99)
Orthodox (6)
Anglicans (7.5)
Other Christians (33)

- Mainly Roman Catholic
- Mainly Protestant
- Protestant & Roman Catholic
- Thinly populated areas

# CLIMATE AND VEGETATION

North America has every kind of climatic and vegetation region. The north is cold, but the United States has large areas of temperate forest and grasslands. Deserts cover parts of the southwestern United States, while southern Mexico, the Caribbean and Central America lie in the hot tropics.

**Typical mountain climate**

Polar

Mountain

Tundra

Coniferous forest

Mixed forest

Broadleaf forest

Evergreen forest

Prairie

Steppe

Savanna

Mediterranean

Dry tropical scrub

Desert

Tropical rainforest

Dry scrub

Monsoon forest

Large areas of western North America have a mountain climate. Mountain climates vary according to the height of the land. The climate at the base of a mountain range may be warm, but the highest peaks have a polar climate.

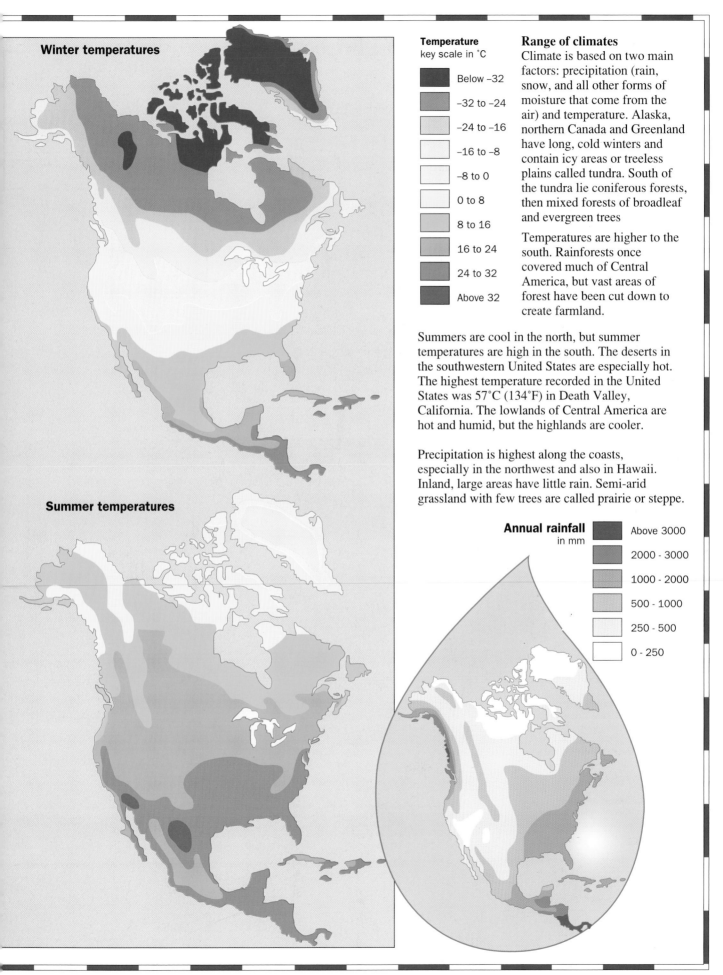

**Winter temperatures**

**Summer temperatures**

**Temperature**
key scale in °C

| | |
|---|---|
| | Below –32 |
| | –32 to –24 |
| | –24 to –16 |
| | –16 to –8 |
| | –8 to 0 |
| | 0 to 8 |
| | 8 to 16 |
| | 16 to 24 |
| | 24 to 32 |
| | Above 32 |

**Range of climates**

Climate is based on two main factors: precipitation (rain, snow, and all other forms of moisture that come from the air) and temperature. Alaska, northern Canada and Greenland have long, cold winters and contain icy areas or treeless plains called tundra. South of the tundra lie coniferous forests, then mixed forests of broadleaf and evergreen trees

Temperatures are higher to the south. Rainforests once covered much of Central America, but vast areas of forest have been cut down to create farmland.

Summers are cool in the north, but summer temperatures are high in the south. The deserts in the southwestern United States are especially hot. The highest temperature recorded in the United States was 57°C (134°F) in Death Valley, California. The lowlands of Central America are hot and humid, but the highlands are cooler.

Precipitation is highest along the coasts, especially in the northwest and also in Hawaii. Inland, large areas have little rain. Semi-arid grassland with few trees are called prairie or steppe.

**Annual rainfall**
in mm

| | |
|---|---|
| | Above 3000 |
| | 2000 - 3000 |
| | 1000 - 2000 |
| | 500 - 1000 |
| | 250 - 500 |
| | 0 - 250 |

# ECOLOGY AND ENVIRONMENT

The land is always changing. Natural forces, such as volcanic eruptions, great storms and unceasing erosion contribute to the change. People also change the land. Human activities cause pollution, while intensive farming exposes the land to the wind and rain, turning former grasslands into desert.

**Greenhouse effect**
Atmosphere
Sun's rays

Waste gases trap more heat

GREENLAND (DENMARK)

ALASKA (US)

Exxon Valdez oil spill 1989

CANADA

Mt St Helens volcano erupts 1980

Three Mile Island nuclear accident 1979

San Francisco earthquake 1906

UNITED STATES

Worst flooding along Mississippi for 300 years 1993

BAHAMAS

Montserrat volcano erupts 1997

DOMINICAN REPUBLIC

CUBA

HAITI

JAMAICA

MEXICO

Mexico City earthquake 1985

BELIZE

Worst floods and landslides for 200 years 1998

GUATEMALA

HONDURAS

EL SALVADOR

NICARAGUA

COSTA RICA

PANAMA

ANTIGUA AND BARBUDA
ST KITTS AND NEVIS
DOMINICA
ST LUCIA
BARBADOS
ST VINCENT AND THE GRENADINES
GRENADA
TRINIDAD AND TOBAGO

## Environmental damage to land and sea

- Area most affected by acid rain
- Existing desert
- Area at risk of desertification
- Present rainforest
- Rainforest seriously damaged in recent years
- Most polluted seas
- Most polluted rivers
- Major environmental disasters

## Damaging the environment

Air pollution is a problem in North America where factories, cars and homes emit waste gases into the air. Some gases dissolve in water vapour and cause acid rain which kills trees. Excess carbon dioxide increases the atmosphere's natural greenhouse effect and may be causing global warming.

The clearing of forests and of grasslands lays soil bare. Strong winds and rain remove the topsoil making the land barren. The destruction of rainforests also threatens many living creatures with extinction.

Water pollution is caused by agricultural chemicals and waste from factories being washed or pumped into rivers and lakes, and by oil spills and untreated sewage at sea. Pollution is also caused by accidents at nuclear power stations. Today, people are working to combat pollution and its deadly effects.

## Natural hazards

Earthquakes are common in western North America and the Caribbean, which lie on unstable parts of the earth's crust. Volcanic eruptions occur in Alaska, Washington, Mexico, Central America and the Caribbean. Hurricanes cause great damage in the Caribbean and the southeastern United States, while violent tornadoes tear through the central plains of the United States. Devastating floods occur when rivers overflow.

**Natural hazards**

Earthquake zones

 Active volcanoes

 Hurricane tracks (June to October)

 Tornado danger areas

## Endangered species

North America was once a vast, mostly empty, wilderness, where many wild animals flourished. But in the last 400 years, hunting and the destruction of natural vegetation have greatly reduced the numbers of animals. Some species are close to extinction.

Fortunately, many endangered species are now protected and some have begun to recover their numbers. Even the bald eagle, symbol of the United States, was threatened, but the US government announced in 1999 that its numbers had recovered sufficiently for it to be removed from the endangered list after 32 years.

California condor

**Some endangered species of North America**

**Birds**
California condor
Eskimo curlew
Ivory-billed woodpecker
Prairie chicken

**Mammals**
American bison
Black bear
Central American tapir
Jaguarundi
Volcano rabbit

**Marine mammals**
Grey whale
Manatee

**Trees**
Caribbean mahogany
Giant sequoia

# ECONOMY

North America is rich in natural resources, including coal, oil, gas and most of the metals used in industry. It also has forests and large areas of fertile farmland. The most developed countries are the United States and Canada. Together, they produce about one-third of the world's industrial goods.

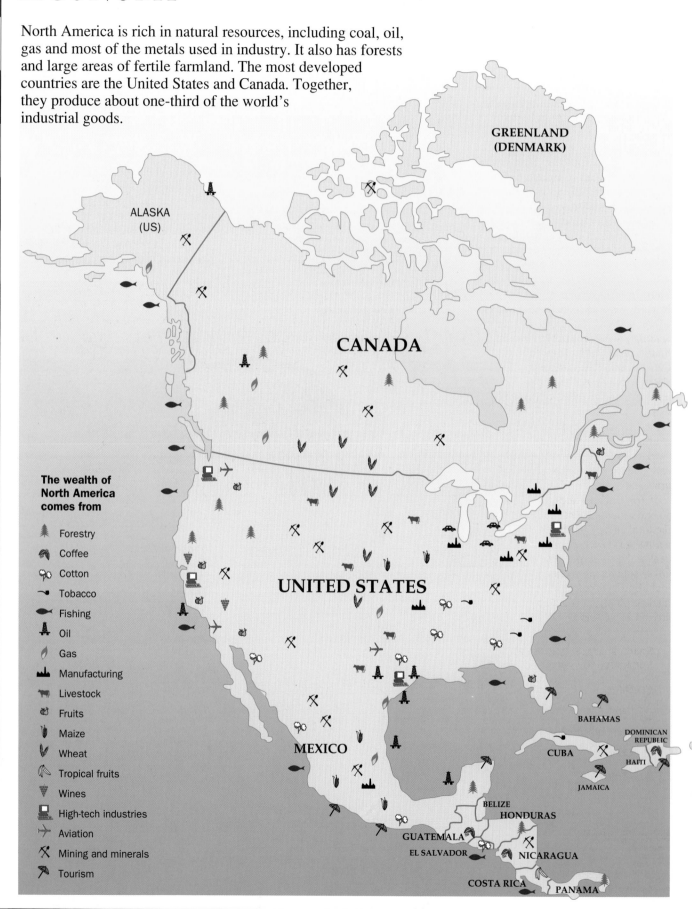

GREENLAND
(DENMARK)

ALASKA
(US)

CANADA

UNITED STATES

MEXICO

BAHAMAS

DOMINICAN
REPUBLIC

CUBA

HAITI

JAMAICA

BELIZE

HONDURAS

GUATEMALA

EL SALVADOR

NICARAGUA

COSTA RICA

PANAMA

**The wealth of North America comes from**

- Forestry
- Coffee
- Cotton
- Tobacco
- Fishing
- Oil
- Gas
- Manufacturing
- Livestock
- Fruits
- Maize
- Wheat
- Tropical fruits
- Wines
- High-tech industries
- Aviation
- Mining and minerals
- Tourism

## Gross national product

In order to compare the economies of countries, experts work out the gross national product (GNP) of the countries in US dollars. The GNP is the total value of all the goods and services produced in a country in a year. The pie chart, right, shows that the GNP of the United States is more than seven times bigger than the combined GNPs of all the other countries in North America. No other country in the world has a higher GNP than the United States.

### GNP for the countries of North America
(in billions of dollars)

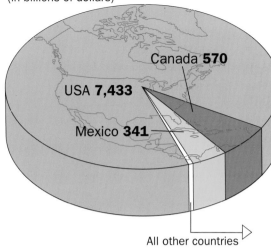

Canada **570**

USA **7,433**

Mexico **341**

All other countries

Cuba **17**
Guatemala **16**
Dominican Republic **12**
El Salvador **10**
Costa Rica **9**
Panama **8**
Trinidad and Tobago **5**
Honduras **4**
Jamaica **4**
Bahamas **3**
Barbados **2**
Haiti **2**
Nicaragua **2**
Belize **0.6**
Antigua and Barbuda **0.5**
St Lucia **0.5**
Grenada **0.3**
Dominica **0.2**
St Kitts and Nevis **0.2**
St Vincent and Grenadines **0.2**

### Per capita GNPs

Per capita means per head or per person. Per capita GNPs are worked out by dividing the GNP by the population. For example, the per capita GNP of the United States is $28,020. Canada has a per capita GNP of $19,020. Poor countries have low per capita GNPs. For example, Haiti has a per capita GNP of only $310.

## Sources of energy

North America produces about a fifth of the world's oil. The leading producer is the United States, followed by Mexico, Canada, and Trinidad and Tobago. North America also produces about a third of the world's natural gas. Hydroelectricity (water power) is important, especially in Canada, while other important energy sources are coal and uranium.

In the United States, oil provides about 39 per cent of the total energy produced, natural gas about 24 per cent and coal 22 per cent. Other sources of energy, including hydroelectric and nuclear plants, account for around 15 per cent.

### Sources of energy found in North America

- 🛢 Oil
- 🝑 Gas
- ≋ Hydroelectricity
- ⚒ Coal
- ☢ Uranium

ANTIGUA AND BARBUDA
ST KITTS AND NEVIS
DOMINICA
ST LUCIA
BARBADOS
ST VINCENT AND THE GRENADINES
GRENADA
TRINIDAD AND TOBAGO

43

# POLITICS AND HISTORY

North America contains 23 independent countries. The United States and Mexico are federal republics. Canada, Belize and eight Caribbean nations are constitutional monarchies. They have their own governments, but they recognize the British monarch as their head of state. Ten countries are democratic republics, while Cuba is a Communist republic. North America also includes 14 overseas territories linked to Britain, Denmark, France, Netherlands and the United States.

**Longships** like these were used by the Vikings to explore the coasts of Greenland and mainland North America a thousand years ago

GREENLAND (DENMARK)

ALASKA (US)

CANADA

UNITED STATES

BAHAMAS

DOMINICAN REPUBLIC

CUBA

HAITI

JAMAICA

MEXICO

BELIZE

GUATEMALA

HONDURAS

EL SALVADOR

NICARAGUA

COSTA RICA

PANAMA

## Great events

The timeline below begins with the arrival of the first people from Asia towards the end of the Great Ice Age. They were the ancestors of the Native Americans.

The modern history of North America began in 1492, when the explorer Christopher Columbus, sailing from Spain, reached the Caribbean Sea. He thought he had reached Asia, but instead he had found a 'New World' unknown to Europeans at that time. Following this discovery, many immigrants settled in North America. The United States declared its independence from Britain in 1776 and subsequently became the most powerful nation on earth.

Today the continent is populated by Native Americans and by many more people of European, African and Asian origin.

### Political system

- Federal republic
- Constitutional monarchy
- Democratic republic
- Communist republic
- Overseas territory

**Important dates**

Early people crossed from Asia and moved south through North America

3000 Pottery being produced in what is now Mexico

1150 Olmec civilization founded in Mexico

550 Mesa Verde in Colorado, USA, built by Pueblo Indians

800 Mayan civilization founded in Central America

1000 Vikings from Greenland reach mainland of North America

1325 Rise of Aztecs in Mexico and the city of Tenochtitlán founded. It later became Mexico City

1492 Christopher Columbus reached 'New W

1493 First Spanish settlers arr North America

1497 John Cab to North A fro

| 10,000 BC | AD 1 | AD 1000 | 1500 |

44

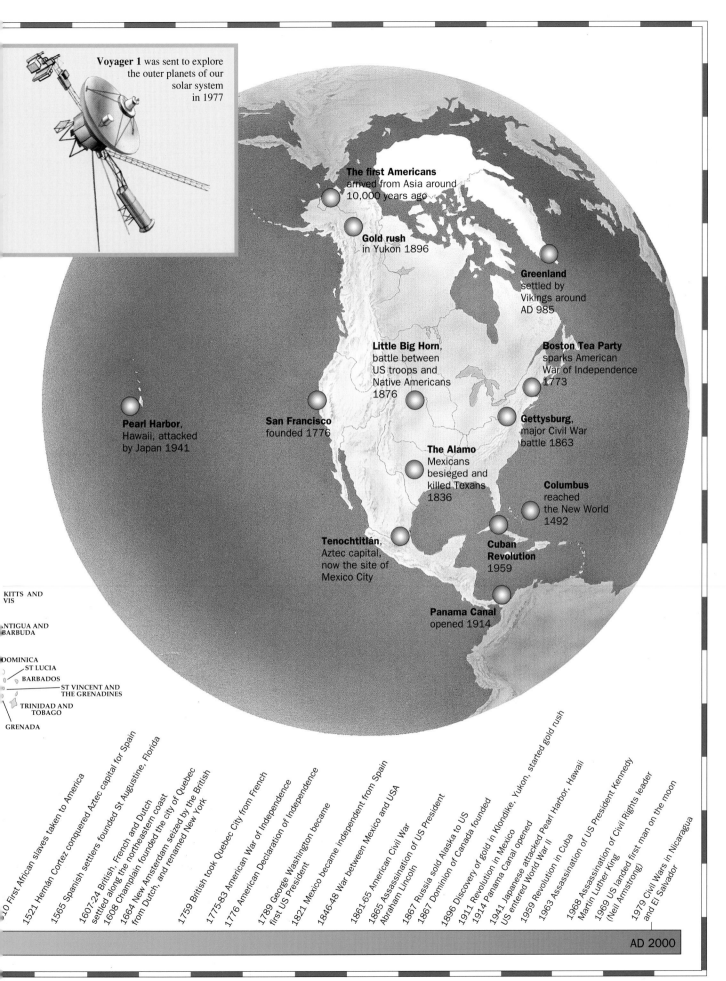

**Voyager 1** was sent to explore the outer planets of our solar system in 1977

**The first Americans** arrived from Asia around 10,000 years ago

**Gold rush** in Yukon 1896

**Greenland** settled by Vikings around AD 985

**Little Big Horn**, battle between US troops and Native Americans 1876

**Boston Tea Party** sparks American War of Independence 1773

**Pearl Harbor**, Hawaii, attacked by Japan 1941

**San Francisco** founded 1776

**Gettysburg**, major Civil War battle 1863

**The Alamo** Mexicans besieged and killed Texans 1836

**Columbus** reached the New World 1492

**Tenochtitlán**, Aztec capital, now the site of Mexico City

**Cuban Revolution** 1959

**Panama Canal** opened 1914

KITTS AND
VIS

NTIGUA AND
BARBUDA

DOMINICA
ST LUCIA
BARBADOS
ST VINCENT AND
THE GRENADINES
TRINIDAD AND
TOBAGO
GRENADA

610 First African slaves taken to America

1521 Hernán Cortez conquered Aztec capital for Spain

1565 Spanish settlers founded St Augustine, Florida

1607-24 British, French and Dutch settled along the northeastern coast

1608 Champlain founded the city of Quebec

1664 New Amsterdam seized by the British from Dutch, and renamed New York

1759 British took Quebec City from French

1775-83 American War of Independence

1776 American Declaration of Independence

1789 George Washington became first US President

1821 Mexico became independent from Spain

1846-48 War between Mexico and USA

1861-65 American Civil War

1865 Assassination of US President Abraham Lincoln

1867 Russia sold Alaska to US

1867 Dominion of Canada founded

1896 Discovery of gold in Klondike, Yukon, started gold rush

1911 Revolution in Mexico

1914 Panama Canal opened

1941 Japanese attacked Pearl Harbor, Hawaii US entered World War II

1959 Revolution in Cuba

1963 Assassination of US President Kennedy

1968 Assassination of Civil Rights leader Martin Luther King

1969 US landed first man on the moon (Neil Armstrong)

1979 Civil Wars in Nicaragua and El Salvador

AD 2000

# INDEX

Numbers in **bold** are map references
Numbers in *italics* are picture references

46

47

**Picture credits**
**Photographs:** Travel Photo International 1, 5, 9, 13, 21, 23, 25, 26, 27, 33, 34
AS Publishing 4, 10, 15
Keith Lye 4, 29